FAT SOUL

A Philosophy of

S-I-Z-E

Fat Soul

Other Works by Patricia Adams Farmer

(Nonfiction)
Embracing a Beautiful God

Replanting Ourselves in Beauty:
Toward an Ecological Civilization (with Jay McDaniel)

(Fiction)
The Metaphor Maker

Fat Soul Fridays

FAT SOUL

A Philosophy of

S-I-Z-E

Patricia Adams Farmer

SHIPROCK PRESS

ISBN -13   978-1523460885
ISBN-10   1523460881

Cover Penguin Baby © by ha kule, Shutterstock Images

"Fat Soul" logo designs by Mathew McDaniel

Dedication

To Ron,
whose wide, wide capacity for love
stretches my soul
every day,
every which way,
and then some.

Table of Contents

Part One
The Beauty of Inner Immensity

Part Two
Fat Soul Planet

Part Three
Fat Soul Luminaries

Part Four
The S-I-Z-E of Hope

Acknowledgements

I am indebted to the late philosopher and theologian Bernard Loomer, whose iconic essay "S-I-Z-E Is the Measure" first sparked my imagination in the direction of Fat Soul. In the spirit of S-I-Z-E, I am grateful beyond measure to Jay McDaniel, Willis Holmes Professor of Religious Studies at Hendrix College, editor of the website *Jesus, Jazz, and Buddhism,* and my collaborator in the development of the many dimensions of Fat Soul. I stand in awe of his on-going creative contribution to Fat Soul thinking, his application of Fat Soul to multi-cultural dialogue and ecological thinking in local communities in the U.S. and beyond, and for his guitar playing in the Fat Soul Band. I am also grateful to those large souls who have influenced and encouraged my writing through the years, including Marjorie Suchocki, David Polk, and Bruce Epperly (a student of Bernard Loomer). I also want to thank all those beautiful Fat Souls from around the world, part of our Fat Soul International community, who have participated in on-line discussions, helping me hone the possibilities of unity within diversity a little better. Above all, I wish to thank my amazing husband of thirty-nine years, Ron Farmer, a professor, writer, and the most generous soul I know.

Prologue

Widening Circles

*I live my life in widening circles
That reach out across the world.
I may not ever complete the last one,
But I give myself to it.*

—Rainer Maria Rilke

This book was written from the fattest place on Earth. That is, for five years, I lived and wrote and entertained Big Thoughts in the equatorial country of Ecuador. At the equator, the earth literally bulges out. Seriously. While the mean radius of Earth is a mere 3,959 miles, at the equator the diameter measures 7,926 miles! Not only that, but Ecuador (including the Galapagos) is, for its size, the most biologically diverse place on earth, whose long lists of species of birds and tree frogs and butterflies and penguins and a million various and sundry creatures could fill up reams of paper in fat, bulging files.

Under the wide blue sky, with incredible beauty and massive diversity at every turn, who could not think deeply and widely? Who could not indulge in unfettered spaciousness? Who could not feel enormously fat with soul-stretching ideas? Ecuador is a place to practice the art of awe, to wonder, to think, and to create. And that is, more or less, what I did for those five years: pondered the many dimensions of what philosopher Bernard Loomer called S-I-Z-E, playing with ideas while staring back at bright green baby iguanas who attached themselves to the screen on my kitchen window.

So it is in this luscious, tropical context, accompanied by my enchantment with trees, my philosophical and theological background, and a wide assortment of neurotic tendencies, that I developed a philosophy which I call Fat Soul—not a philosophy in the tradition sense, but one created out of story and experience and love. At the same time, way up in Arkansas, Professor Jay McDaniel of Hendrix College, joined me in working out many fresh and lively dimensions of Fat Soul philosophy with transforming possibilities for both individuals and communities. We believe that Fat Soul is a playful—and yes, culturally edgy—metaphor which seeks to counter rigid, fearful, and thin-thinking worldviews that currently endanger both peace and planetary well-being.

It can also save one's sanity in a pinch.

At the middle of the world, I also happened to be at the middle of my life (Okay, perhaps a tad to the right of middle). Midlife, broadly speaking, is a time when we struggle with meaning and regrets and our own mortality; we feel the urgency to expand our souls in fresh explorations. We also have the opportunity to finally make peace with our inner demons; and if we're lucky, we discover how to integrate them lovingly into something larger and more transforming and meaningful than we could ever imagine at an earlier age.

It is my hope that younger generations can benefit from the struggles and wide wisdom of those of us in middle years and beyond, even while creating and expanding their own souls in the challenging new world they have inherited. Fat Soul is a vision of life meant especially for them—for the future.

My hope, too, is that this book will speak to people of various faiths, traditions, and spiritual preferences. While I happen to be a progressive Christian (with multi-faith proclivities), the truth is that Fat Soul does not belong to any one religion or tradition; it is simply too fat.

That's the whole point of Fat Soul. Fat Soul is a philosophy of life that embraces the width and depth and beauty of our interconnectedness. That's why I have Fat Soul friends who are Catholic, Jewish, Evangelical, Buddhist, Muslim, Mormon, Atheist, and Nothing-In-Particular. As a hospitable philosophy, Fat Soul welcomes religious pluralism with open arms. Like the country of Ecuador, which sits on the bulging equator basking in the gladness of its diversity, so, too, Fat Soul finds its truest, most full-bodied gladness in the beauty of multiplicity.

Fat Soul philosophy can then serve as a kind of wide-angle lens through which to examine life, love, meaning, and spirituality. But Fat Soul is not just a lot of abstract head-talk, but rather mirrors actual life: it is shot through with feeling; it is earthy and active and poetic and whimsical and messy. It is never quite finished, and has a penchant for improvisation. It dares to cross borders, to speak new languages, to color outside the lines, and to laugh and play and think and dream and form rock bands.

If the word "fat" is just too existentially painful for you—I hear you—Fat Soul can also be thought of as an acronym: F-flexible, A-aesthetic, T-tender. These three words make up the essence of Fat Soul thinking. That is, a Flexible-Aesthetic-Tender Soul (F.A.T. Soul, if you will) chooses flexibility over rigidity to deal with the realities of change; it values an aesthetic of intense harmonies–diversified forms of beauty—over sameness; and it responds to the world with tenderness and compassion rather than control and coercion.

You will also see in these pages the name Alfred North Whitehead mentioned extensively, if not ex-cessively. That's because the great British philosopher and mathematician (1861-1947) is the intellectual father of Fat Soul philosophy. That is, he believed in a Flexible-Aesthetic-Tender sort of philosophy. I discovered Whitehead's "philosophy of organism"—also called "process philosophy"—in graduate school at the

University of Missouri and shortly thereafter started gaining girth in my soul. In particular, his startlingly fresh—if not subversive—view of God, power, and reality itself upended my slim worldview and set me on a soulful path as a Fat Soul philosopher (more about this in the Epilogue).

NOTE: You absolutely do not have to rush to the library to find the works of Whitehead in order to understand Fat Soul philosophy. In fact, I would caution against it unless you feel particularly drawn to this area of study. You have heard of tortured artists; well, there are also tortured philosophers. Most of these are Whiteheadians. I've done the suffering for you, so just relax and enjoy the ride.

Now, a word about God. While not all Fat Souls (or religions) entertain an idea of God, I admit that I gladly, exuberantly, and without apology embrace Whitehead's God: a Flexible-Aesthetic-Tender sort of God, a God who is affected by our choices, who seeks always after beauty, and who "dwells in the tender elements of the world . . ." I continue to be smitten by this God of love and beauty and tenderness, which works well with my progressive religious faith. Still, this may not be your cup of tea. It's okay—really. You can enjoy Fat Soul philosophy in your own way, expanding and creating fresh meaning from the perspective of your own tradition.

So, then, with all our differences taken into account, what does it really mean to be a Fat Soul (or F.A.T. Soul) and why does it matter?

To be a Fat Soul simply means that we are willing to let go of the rigid, false borders that alienate us from each other and from the earth and within our own psyches. It is to let go of self-righteousness and absolutism and mindsets based on fear; in this way, Fat Soul can serve as an antidote to fundamentalism.

To be a Fat Soul is to embrace a wider, more elastic sense of self based on the reality of our profound interconnection in the web of life; it is to live deeply, expansively, imaginatively, and courageously. Best of all, a Fat Soul philosophy of life dares us, despite these difficult times, to be stubbornly and undauntedly drenched in delight. As the celebrated writer Elizabeth Gilbert says, "Only when we are at our most playful can divinity finally get serious with us."[1]

To be a Fat Soul is to stretch toward this wider beauty, which includes not only intense delight, but also intense caring for the darkness—and there is much of that in our hearts and in the world. This means we must first make plenty of room in the soul for self-compassion, especially for the shadowy and broken parts that need space and caring in order to be transformed; then we are free to widen the circle of compassion to include friends and strangers and trees and cows and the whole wide earth. We are all connected, we all deserve compassion. We all belong.

So, you see, there is no litmus test for Fat Soulhood—except, perhaps, for kindness. You can spot a Fat Soul from a mile away simply by an act of kindness. For in its essence, Fat Soul is a metaphor for inclusiveness, hospitality, and generosity of spirit. It is a way to think about our spirituality in terms of listening– deeply, and without judgment–to those who are different from us. A spirituality of S-I-Z-E, then, challenges us not only to plumb the riches within our own beloved faith tradition or worldview, but to move out beyond our little circles of sameness for the sake of beauty, love, and our very survival on this imperiled planet.

In the following pages, you will find personal reflections on a philosophy of S-I-Z-E based on my own experiences as a Fat Soul philosopher living abroad, and living *broadly*. Each piece was written at a different time and in different contexts during my sojourn. Not every piece will reflect the landscape of Ecuador, but still, Ecuador's diversity, beauty, and raw natural setting nourished my creativity while its challenges and heartbreaks forced lazy muscles in my soul to finally wake up and start working. Each writing was in itself a way to expand a little further into some realm of insight that helped my soul grow a little plumper and rounder and more flexible and forgiving. So this book is for you, but I confess that it was written first of all for me, for my own survival in a strange land.

Earlier versions of these reflections have appeared on the website *Jesus, Jazz, and Buddhism*. A few of these reflections have also appeared in the anthology, *Replanting Ourselves in Beauty*.[2]   Now they appear together, in expanded form, as pieces that belong to a single whole and are offered up like slices of a multi-layered cake, say, German chocolate—or Italian cream, if that's your thing.

All calories are free in the realm of Fat Soul.

After reading this book, I hope you will join our Fat Soul International community. Yes, we even have a Manifesto! (See "For Further Expansion" at the end of this book.)   Join our discussion groups online, and perhaps even share your own story, adding yet another widening circle "that reaches out across the world."

Part One

The Beauty of
Inner Immensity

How Big Is Your Soul?

Practice any art, music, singing, dancing, acting, drawing, painting, sculpting, poetry, fiction, essays, reportage, no matter how well or badly, not to get money and fame, but to experience <u>becoming</u>, to find out what's inside you, <u>to make your soul grow</u>.

–Kurt Vonnegut

"How big is your soul?"

Professor Bernard Loomer (1912-1985), a towering figure in process theology, used to toss out this question in his public lectures like a mantra, a challenge, a sort of summing up of everything that matters. I think it might just be the most important question we can ask ourselves. I still remember the day as a young philosophy grad student when I encountered his essay titled "S-I-Z-E Is the Measure" in a big book called *Religious Experience and Process Theology:*

> By S-I-Z-E I mean the stature of [your] soul, the range and depth of [your] love, [your] capacity for relationships. I mean the volume of life you can take into your being and still maintain your integrity and individuality, the intensity and variety of outlook you can entertain in the unity of your being without feeling defensive or insecure. I mean the strength of your spirit to encourage others to become freer in the development of their diversity and uniqueness. I mean the power to sustain more complex and enriching tensions. I

mean the magnanimity of concern to provide conditions that enable others to increase in stature.[3]

I shut the fat book with a huge smile and thought I had found nirvana. At the very least, I had found an idea that took root in my soul and began to grow—to take on S-I-Z-E.

Loomer's words grew and grew inside me through the years, becoming fatter and fatter, something like The Blob (as in the 1958 movie)—only friendlier. Finally, there was no more room for it in my brain: I had to create characters to live it out for me in novels. But such fatness spills over to real life, too, as I write essays about "Big Ideas," ideas that might feel uncomfortable to people of "thin thinking." Like how rocks are alive and how trees can talk back and how the heart of God is so big and deep and wide that it feels the sufferings of all creation. All of this sounds a little crazy, like a shaman—which is exactly why Professor Jay McDaniel aptly calls it: Fat Soul Shamanism.[4]

But what is Fat Soul philosophy? For that matter, what is the soul? When you think of the soul, what image comes to mind? A huge white mass of ghost-like ether inside of you? Think again, this time in terms of a process-relational view of the world. The philosophy of Alfred North Whitehead dispelled the whole "ghost in the machine" view of identity. In fact, he dispelled the modern mechanistic worldview altogether! As far as metaphors go, machines are out; flowing rivers are in. Professor Bob Mesle gives us a particularly lovely metaphor for the soul when he conducted a wedding. He said to the couple:

> I am a philosopher, let me tell you a great secret of life—a soul is not a thing, it is not something which stands untouched by the events of your life. Your soul is the river of your life; it is the cumulative flow of your experience. But what

do we experience? The world. Each other. So your soul is the cumulative flow of all of your relationships with everything and everyone around you.[5]

So then, if our souls are the cumulative flow of all of our relationships with everything and everyone around us, that's one huge river. But why not just call it a big soul? Why *fat* soul? Who wants to be fat? Isn't fat a bad word?

This is the *subversive* side of Fat Soul. A merely big soul sounds benign and friendly even to mainstream thinking, but the term Fat Soul is edgy, for the Fat Soul dares to get bigger than society deems proper. Think, for example, of our fashion culture, how it deifies the thin woman. I find the Tyranny of Thin to be highly irritating and sometimes unhealthy—even deadly. I used to teach young women who were dying of starvation, barely able to pick up a textbook, let alone to think. These women with anorexia nervosa were sensitive and smart and perfectionists: a lethal combination in the face of the Tyranny of Thin.

But of course we're not talking about the physical body, but rather the psyche, the soul, the river of experiences that makes up who we are. Yet the same tyranny exists. We are supposed to be focused on wealth and success while keeping "us" and "them" categories neat and tidy. In terms of power relations, we are not supposed to think too much about sharing power, for shared power is entirely too fat! Neither are we to waste too much brain power on "the least of these" or the threatened bee population or the way the seas are rising or how gays must feel when denied a marriage license or how Muslims must feel when Westerners demonize them. That's getting a bit fat in our thinking, isn't it? Go back to thin thinking! It's so much easier. Keep the focus on money, unilateral power, us-versus-them, and the belief that we are wholly separate from nature. Yes, let's keep our thinking thin.

All the while we are a world dying of anorexia nervosa of the spirit.

Yet, as Loomer reminds us, even while enlarging our souls there are limits to what we can take in, for we are not God. The truth is that we are small and flawed and fear things that we don't understand. But we can embrace even that, can't we? We can love and accept ourselves even in our limitations—for we are not, in reality, human *beings*, but rather human *becomings*. And we can *become* bigger, even if just a little bit.

All you really have to remember about Fat Soul is that a Fat Soul is a beautiful soul. In the process worldview, God is the very Soul of the world, the ultimate instance of The Fat Soul, the One who lures us and all creation toward widening circles of beauty. God yearns for beautiful relationships of earth and sky and people and turtles. God yearns for us to know that we are all of a piece, all deeply interwoven and wholly beautiful in our differences.

But aren't we afraid of losing ourselves in the process of widening our circles of empathy and understanding? A Fat Soul philosophy would say that striving for a bigger soul does not diminish one's own identity, uniqueness, or beauty; rather, it strengthens individual identity and uniqueness and beauty in the way a single color is brought to life in a painting by the splash of a contrasting color next to it.

Beauty is all about intensity of feeling, the kind that emerges from mutual relationships of respect and reverence and tenderness. Beauty thrives on contrasts and differences for the sake of intense harmonies—and that, after all, is what makes the world go round. As one of my fictional characters, a philosopher named Madeline, says to her little flock of tea drinkers and thinkers in *Fat Soul Fridays*: "A beautiful soul is a large soul, one that can overcome the smallness and pettiness of our human condition. A really fat soul can welcome diverse people, ideas, and ways of being in the world without feeling threatened. A fat soul experiences the intensity of life in its fullness, even the painful side of life, and knows there is something still bigger . . ."[6]

S-I-Z-I-N-G Up

Daring to expand the soul in a soul-shrinking world of Us and Them is nothing less than counter-cultural. It is a form of protest against the dangerous trend of thin-thinking that impoverishes individuals, communities, the planet, and the very Soul of the world. A beautiful soul, a large soul, is the result of careful and courageous creativity. Creativity drives this world, this cosmos, for every moment is a moment of becoming, of creativity, and we are all invited to the party. The writer Kurt Vonnegut believed that creativity can grow the soul, that it can help us in the process of becoming. This is a very Whiteheadian notion, and I believe it's true; it has helped me grow my own soul. You don't have to be a writer or an artist to do this. All of life is creativity—every choice is a co-creation with the divine. Those who choose to live creativity and largely know this instinctively. Let go of the things that make your soul contract. Create something with your life today, and do it with gladness. The world seems hell-bent on making us miserable and afraid. Resist. Go wide. It's time to lighten up and get fat.

The Meaning of Success Revisited

Because our value is a gift, we don't have to prove ourselves, only to express ourselves, and what a world of difference there is between proving ourselves and expressing ourselves.
—William Sloan Coffin

At some point in midlife, we confront the inevitable what's-it-all-about-Alfie moment. We question everything we've done and everything we are and everything we want to be. Even the great ones do it, like Anne Morrow Lindbergh who said, "There comes a moment when the things one has written, even a traveler's memories, stand up and demand a justification. They require an explanation. They query, 'Who am I? What is my name? Why am I here?'"

These are good questions, but for most Westerners our automatic pilot tends to be stuck on: How much have I earned? How does this compare with my peers? What about status? Awards? Applause? On a more virtuous note, we comb through our pasts looking for some solid, statistical evidence that we did in fact "make a difference." As we look back, we automatically rack up our life accomplishments like billiard balls, each one round and shiny and solid. They have a pleasant sound when they click together, like a community of self-congratulation.

But now, on the downside of the half-century mark, I've come to think about all this differently. The problem with racking up our accomplishments in terms of outward success is that no matter how many billiard balls of achievement we rack up, it is never enough. Never. There is always someone right next to us who has done way better and there are those who have done far worse, so we are caught between painful jealousy and smug arrogance. Not to mention, those seemingly solid trophies and accolades don't generally last anyway, as racked balls eventually disappear from the table, one by one, into the black holes of history.

At this time in my life I think about such things, especially now that I have retired from my day job. But retirement comes with a price. I have discovered that when life slows down and the outer clutter is cleared away, the bullies from the basement of the mind take this as an invitation to step into the limelight with, "Ah, so we're finally alone! Well, how did you stack up? What have you got to show for yourself?" And then marches in the What Might Have Beens and the Should Haves and the If Onlys.

This is torture, not what I signed up for when clearing my schedule.

These taunting, ill-mannered basement people are not our best selves, but skulk up from the shadowy depths and prowl about the mind. They really get going about 3:00 a.m. when resistance is futile, but they are known to barge in at any time, especially when we're tired and discouraged. They lecture us on what a total failure we have been and *if only* we had done this or that. These uninvited guests are rude, crude, and socially unattractive. I don't want to listen to them, so I try to watch television or read a book. But then I remembered that Jesus entertained publicans and sinners, so the least I can do is listen. And learn. Ironically, these inner bullies can also be backdoor friends, for by the discontent they stir up in our psyches, they force us to re-evaluate and question and find a larger harmony within our souls.

There's no getting around it. At some point we need to confront these ill-mannered guests squarely until we understand the deep wounds they represent. If we don't acknowledge them and give them their due, they will run wild, raid the fridge, invite other lowlifes in for beer and pizza and leave the place a wreck. So we approach them with a calming cup of tea, a little mindfulness, a little prayer, a little meditation, and many, many, many pages of journaling. This is how I do it, anyway. Having confronted the rude guests one by one, I know that I am enlarging my soul by learning to invite in the unsavory as well as the pleasant, to face and forgive, and to think differently about the meaning of life.

In my inner dialogue with these serenity crashers—the If Onlys in particular—I have discovered the curious power of perspective. I mean, when you're looking backwards at your life of over half a century, the whole picture looks different. Totally. Like a parable of Jesus—the way he would stand things on their heads—tiny mustard seeds getting the limelight, or the poor inheriting the earth. It's like that, a discombobulation of everything formerly understood as *the way it is*. Suddenly, I see so clearly at this age what I never could grasp before, the startling wisdom that the only truly important accomplishments in life are the accomplishments of the soul.

I am tempted to think that this "aha!" moment is something brand new, but Carl Jung was on to this years ago when he identified and analyzed this unsettling midlife passage. Jung said that the first half of life is all about developing a "persona" for the outer world—wearing different masks so that we fit in—while the second half is about peeling back the persona in search of the "true individual." The goal, he said, is to transcend our ego and become more authentic, a kind of "widening out" or being more "rounded." In this view, midlife is a metamorphosis—the sloughing off what binds us in order to refine or rethink or even dramatically rebirth ourselves.

If we peer into the meaning of midlife, everything inverts. We judge ourselves with a whole new rubric, the rubric of the soul—that growing, blossoming authentic self that gets short shrift in the madness of competition.

We move from the pressure to prove ourselves to the freedom of expressing ourselves. We switch from "how big is my bank account?" to "how big is my soul?" We learn to embrace the "roundedness" of ourselves (which for many of us includes accepting a more rounded physicality, too). We learn to befriend the dark corners, to integrate, to understand, to accept, and, finally, to love—yes, love—the whole complicated muddle that we are. We begin to grow up and forgive and let go, and most importantly, we see this inner work as the mark of true success—something that can't be racked up and measured, but can be felt and experienced as nothing short of spaciousness.

Now it all seems so obvious! It's all about the soul. And clearly, some of our greatest soulful accomplishments happen in the aftermath of abject failure because we are forced to reckon with ourselves and face our demons with courage. At such crisis points, unwelcomed questions arise that require us to flex our spiritual muscles and grow in self-compassion. Conversely, winning a prestigious award might shrink our soul if we choose to put too much importance on it and forget we are but dust.

It's not that outward success is unimportant. We need to celebrate and savor the moments of "Wow—I did this!" if that success is an expression of our best selves and not a way to prove our value or impress others or beat the competition. The pathological need to prove our value is universal and human and seemingly mandatory in a highly competitive society, but does not come from the true self. It is an ill-conceived story; it is a lie. Our true, spiritual selves tell a different story of how our value is already there, intrinsic—a divine imprint of unconditional love and acceptance that no sin can erase and no achievement can improve upon. We are deeply, completely, and eternally loved by the very Soul of the world. This is our true story. Start with this premise, and everything begins to widen out in joy.

This divinely drenched part of our nature—our creative, ripening, widening-out soul—would ask about the achievements of the inner life. Has my soul grown bigger and more resilient in the face of life's disappointments? Or has it shrunk back in fear? What about the quality of my relationships? Have I learned to forgive? To embrace life with gratitude? To be mindful of the darkness within, and care for it with compassion? Is my capacity for love bigger or smaller? Am I being myself or what someone else wants me to be? Am I trying to express myself or impress others? How am I adding beauty to the world?

This last question is important. I have come to the conclusion that the larger purpose of life has to do with adding some small measure of beauty to the world, something of our own, something of ourselves—an expression of who we really are. Philosopher Alfred North Whitehead says, "The teleology of the Universe is directed toward the production of Beauty."[7] He says that beauty is the dream of God in the world—and that we are the co-creators of such beauty. In this sense, beauty is much wider and deeper and more cosmic than the usual sense of the word. Beauty is not good bone structure, but rather how we create our lives out of the bones and structures that we have been given.

The result of stretching toward beauty is this: One morning we find that our souls have become so large that they randomly burst with gratitude at the sound of a blackbird singing in a tree outside our window. In fact, we don't see much difference between ourselves and the blackbird and the tree, as the planet with all its creatures becomes a kind of extension of our own soul. Our own bodies become temples of Soul, worthy of respect and care.

Once our soul gets this big, it breaks the belt of ego constriction—and when this happens we become less self-conscious, less concerned with what people think of us, less given to racking up our value in terms of what we have achieved or the way we look or how much money we have. The If Onlys and the Should Haves and the What Might Have Beens lose their power and slink back down to the basement, leaving us free and unfettered. The complicated past is sorted out and forgiven; the future, fresh and open. Letting go of the need to prove ourselves leaves us firmly planted in the present, ready to spread our branches up and out into the wide blue spacious sky.

S-I-Z-I-N-G Up

The widening of the soul for the sake of beauty is at the heart of Fat Soul philosophy. The size of the soul matters in this inverted sort of world where it is never too late to be a success at what really counts. Of course, this goes against the grain of everything we've been taught—like Jesus, who absolutely refused to turn stones into bread to impress the devil. He wasn't interested in proving anything, but rather in expressing his own unique self. What if we gave up our need prove ourselves and gave ourselves over to expressing our true selves? What if we taught this to our children and grandchildren? What could be a better goal in life but to increase the size our soul? To add a measure of beauty to the world? To become Fat Souls? When it comes down to it, that's all that really matters. Everything else is just dessert.

A Life in a Day

Each day is a little life; every waking and rising a little birth; every fresh morning a little youth; every going to rest and sleep a little death.
—Arthur Schopenhauer

The perfect moment is fadeless in the lapse of time. Time has then lost its character of 'perpetual perishing'; it becomes the 'moving image of eternity.'
—Alfred North Whitehead

It's a beautiful morning in Ecuador. The equatorial sun pushes itself skyward, edging out the twelve-hour darkness as if saying, STEP ASIDE, PLEASE (or rather, *perdóname, por favor*). The next twelve hours promise verdant green landscapes and skies of celeste blue. Today my husband and I leave our tiny fishing village and travel to the capital of the province to load up on needed supplies for our home and pantry.

The trip takes over two hours and our list is huge and time is short—only twelve hours of sunlight every day, year round. I anticipate a mad-dash sprint around hardware stores, grocery stores, and various *tiendas*. As we open the door to greet our driver, I'm struck by a bright scarlet flower in the background—a vermillion red to be precise—the first hibiscus bloom on our new plant. The bloom captures me somehow, as if it wants to say something to me. But I don't have time to listen.

As we drive through the countryside on our way to battle—the battle against time itself—I have time to think.

My mind returns to the happy bloom, the way it seems to celebrate its own existence in a quiet, unhurried way. I think of how the blooms on the hibiscus bush last only for a single day and then they are gone. One day: then it's over. For the hibiscus bloom, each day is a little life.

I also can't help but think of Whitehead's philosophy, how life is perpetually dying and rebirthing itself, a universe of constant becomings—and what this means to a person, a flower, a universe. And how God "dwells in the tender elements of the world."[8] I also think of the Japanese *mono no aware*, the gentle sadness of things passing away. I feel that wistfulness now.

But I have to stop philosophizing over the ephemeral nature of existence as I have to engage myself in the quest for beating time to get through all the items on our list. I wonder how we can do it in a day—buy all these things!—and time-pressure makes my heart race and my adrenaline flow and my feet stumble and my face take on that shopper's look of quiet desperation.

In the late afternoon, after the exhausting aftermath of victory over time, I slump back into the backseat and grab a water bottle and peanuts—there had been no time for lunch—and stare blankly out the window as villages aglow in recumbent sunshine sweep by me. But as the car slows down to meet the demands of the pocked road, I am captured by a scene that seems to stop time: a woman, a lovely woman, with a glossy black braid and simple print dress, leans languorously over an old wooden balcony above a shop, gazing wistfully down at the street, the hub of her town. She might have looked exactly the same a hundred years ago, for not much has changed in this village. She watches the people below buying vegetables and coconuts on the street, men of business gesticulating their opinions to one another, children—still in school uniforms—sitting on curbs in companionable huddles with melting ice cream bars.

The village is dusty and poor by North American standards, but its inhabitants appear richly happy and vividly alive. They seem to care less about time; they are too busy living. And watching. Ecuadorians love to sit and watch, just like this woman on her balcony. Her hand rests under her chin, as one thinking and imagining and dreaming. Behind her, a vermillion curtain, the very color of a hibiscus bloom, moves and sways soothingly in the warm afternoon breeze. She is an arresting presence, this woman on her *balcón*: a monument to stillness against a moving world, like a Buddhist monk in meditation. She is one who watches things, as if this were the only day she had in the world.

I think back to the fragile hibiscus flower at my own *casa*, how its life must be nearing its end by now: it began in morning gladness as it opened up to the novelty of existence—soon to make conversation with a hummingbird, for hummingbirds flirt wildly with the color red. In the early afternoon, the strong ocean breeze would make the delicate petals flutter and sway, much like the vermillion curtain in the window; and by now, it must be blazing out its color in one last, intense dazzle before closing its petals to evening darkness—and forever.

We don't quite make it home before dark. By the time we lug all our things inside our *casa* and pay the driver, the flower is gone, folded gracefully in death. I missed it. I wonder what else I missed. Then it dawns on me what the hibiscus blossom was trying to say to me all day. It tried hard to break through my frantic feelings of getting things, finding things, buying things. It whispered, too, in the vermillion curtain as it swayed, and in the woman's stillness on her *balcón*. But now I can hear it clearly, that ancient warning: "*Momento mori*," it says. "Remember, you shall die." Long ago these words chastened swaggering Roman soldiers after a victory over their enemies. Their slaves would whisper it in their ears: *momento mori*. It humbled them; it humbles me now in my own Pyrrhic victory over time.

We live as though time were something to beat, as if it is against us—the enemy—something apart from us, demanding and relentless: the Evil Time Troll scowling down on us with a stopwatch in hand. But we are mistaken. Time is not the OTHER; it unfolds as we unfold. Time is a river of becomings alongside the hibiscus bloom and the vermillion curtain and the woman who dreams.

Making peace with time is not just a matter of slowing down; hummingbirds dart and fly about at a dizzying pace but they don't miss the red flower, do they? It is more a matter of making friends with time, with who we are in the moment, whether we are a dizzy hummingbird or a quiet bloom. Instead of racing against the enemy, Time, we could be embracing the vividness of our becomings in the flow of experience. Instead of thinking that we are now living "a day in a life," perhaps we should reverse it and think of ourselves as living "a life in day." Maybe then we could capture something of the vibrancy and significance and fragility of each becoming moment.

And it matters, all this capturing and savoring and feeling the pathos of impermanence. It matters because our becomings flow into the everlasting memory in God. How we pay attention to a flower—the quality of our awareness—becomes an object for the world's next becoming. "The perfect moment is fadeless in the lapse of time." Whitehead would say that I can feel with the flower and imagine it from the inside because it is part of me and I a part of it: this is the interwovenness of life. Together we are forever "perpetually perishing" and yet making an immortal imprint on the whole.

Such is the wisdom of the hibiscus that blooms and dances and perishes under the equatorial sun with perfect equanimity. The river does not bear stepping into twice; the bloom of today will never return in exactly the same way. Time is how we create ourselves in each moment. We are time unfolding, blooming, dying.

Every day is a little life.

S-I-Z-I-N-G Up

Ecuadorians teach us to luxuriate in the spaciousness of Time. The soul needs this nourishment to grow, the kind of richness of experience that comes by paying attention. So, go ahead: embody the moment, and feel your soul begin to blossom.

Inhabit Your Situation

Caretake this moment.
Immerse yourself in its particulars.
Respond to this person, this challenge, this deed.
Quit the evasions.
Stop giving yourself needless trouble.
It is time to really live; to fully inhabit the situation you happen to be in now.
You are not some disinterested bystander.
Exert yourself.

–Epictetus

Epictetus was a Stoic philosopher, and for the Stoics, life was all about the art of living. They valued personal choice and responsibility above everything. Of course, it's all a bit awkward, since the Stoics also believed strongly in Fate, which is of course wholly inconsistent with freewill. Many of us today would conclude that metaphysics was not their strong suit—but they did leave us a great legacy. That is, they *lived* their philosophy rather than just talked about it, something we postmodern know-it-alls could learn from today.

For after all, the Greek and Roman Stoics were of a practical bent; they were born to teach people how to live in the real world, how to respond with integrity, courage, and kindness in the face of life's constant changes and traumas. They saw the outer world as something like a vast and temperamental ocean, utterly outside one's influence and control, and the inner world of the intellect and spirit as the helm of a ship, steering skillfully on a moody and unpredictable sea.

Now I Understand

I admire the audacity of Epictetus to create his own inner serenity in the face of his outer powerlessness as a slave in the all-controlling Roman Empire. He was finally freed after Nero's death only to be banished from Rome by Emperor Domitian (along with all the other philosophers). There he was, an intellectual, a teacher, a philosopher, and yet he had little control over his life. Epictetus' daily life hinged entirely on the vicissitudes of the Empire and the whims and moods of its emperors. While he could not control the outside world or his ailing body (he was disabled), he could change what went on inside his soul. This is where he shines. Epictetus, if alive today, would surely endorse the Serenity Prayer—and definitely embrace Viktor Frankl's philosophy of life built around the fundamental freedom: to choose one's attitude in any set of circumstances.

Epictetus taught his students to "inhabit the situation," whatever it is. Don't live in denial or pro-crastinate or run away screaming. *Inhabit the situation.* If you think you can't do a thing, do it anyway. Epictetus would also applaud Eleanor Roosevelt's famous dictum: "You gain strength, courage and confidence by every experience in which you really stop to look fear in the face. You are able to say to yourself, 'I have lived through this horror. I can take the next thing that comes along.' You must do the thing you think you cannot do."

In my case, doing "the thing you think you cannot do" was learning to be a caregiver in the face of my husband's illness, an illness that left him in need of 24/7 care for a good length of time. This was my first time in a caregiver's role, and I confess, I trembled. I trembled with fear and frustration and a sense of woeful inadequacy. Yet, this was my calling: inhabit the situation, exert myself beyond what I thought I could do physically, and manage the practical day-to-day—practical, not being my forte. As a retired minister, I'm more of the "let us pray" kind of helper. But this situation necessitated that I roll up my cuffs and wade into the unfamiliar. Living in Ecuador, with its different customs and language and hospital protocol—and being far from family—did not add to my comfort.

So, in the beginning, fear inhabited me; that is, until I learned to inhabit the situation. Most challenging of all, I had to deal with my own frightened, rebellious inner child who gets totally ticked off at life's unjust surprises. Feelings arose inside me that were not me—not my best self, anyway—and yet, they needed attention. If I was to take care of my husband, I had to take care of myself, too. I had two patients: my inner child who was silently screaming about how all this totally sucks, and my husband, the actual patient. I had to journal. I had to breathe. I had to pray. I had to reach out to others. I had to practice mindfulness.

Now I understand. I understand, for the first time, what caregivers really go through. I understand the pain and frustration of seeing a loved one suffer, and the inner terror of the "what ifs," and ultimately the inner rage at the whole situation—feelings that bubble up inside every caregiver. I understand how fear can take over and inhabit your mind, and that the only way to deal with it is to widen the soul enough to make room for it, and care for it. It is to say to yourself, "There, there. It's all right to feel this way. Now, can we please get busy?"

So, in fits and starts, I became a student of Epictetus, trying to steer things in the right direction on a very dark and scary sea. *Caretake the moment*, says Epictetus. *Immerse yourself in its particulars. Respond to this person, this challenge, this deed.*

This is good philosophy; it is good because it works. My own philosophy, which springs from Whitehead's process philosophy, is certainly not deterministic like Stoicism, but it dovetails with Epictetus' thinking in that it, too, is practical. It works when the chips are down—especially when it comes to the validation of feelings and the raw truth that life often sucks. Even God thinks so.

The Great Companion

I am not speaking of the traditional God of the philosophers. The all-controlling God "up there" who rules the world in mysterious ways doesn't cut it when you're watching someone you love suffer. A process view suggests a God who actually *inhabits* our suffering. Alfred North Whitehead wrote about a God who is "the great companion—the fellow-sufferer who understands."9 God inhabits the situation. Like a Zen master; like Jesus; like a mother large with child; like water inhabiting the ocean. You just can't separate yourself from the love of God because God is not "up there" pulling strings, but rather lovingly at work in the earth, in your body, in the wind, inside cells and molecules and quarks, inside the numbered hairs on your head and the flowers that toil and spin not. God inhabits the world, yet is more than the world. Inhabiting the situation is what God does, for God, according to Whitehead, is the very Soul of the world.

God, the Soul of the world, does not cause—or "allow"—pain and suffering for some higher good; rather, God embraces the pain with tenderness, and lures the diseased body toward whatever kind of healing is possible in the moment. At the same time, this divine embrace of suffering helps terrified caregivers like me find a way through the trembling.

And sometimes, when we've done all we can do, and prayed all the prayers of heaven and earth, and still there is no progress, we need to let go and trust in God's creative, transforming love to weave even this tragedy into a wider beauty. For it's all about love, that is, the power of love. Sometimes there is nothing but this to sustain us—nothing but the *inhabitation* of Cosmic Love.

S-I-Z-I-N-G Up

The Soul of the world needs a partner, namely, you. And me. And the stars. We are all in this together.

In our interconnected cosmos, we affect God's work in the world and literally change the world with every thought we think, every gesture we make. Fat Soul philosophy does not portray a God defined by power, but rather a God defined by love—or to borrow theologian David Polk's phrase, "the God of empowering love."[10] Thus being *empowered*, there is no place for disinterested bystanders—whether it is in caring for a person, or standing up for justice, or creating sustainable communities for future generations. Personal responsibility—including the inner tasks of prayer and mindfulness—will ever be our calling, even when we have to do what we think we cannot do.

The Art of Savoring

He who kisses the joy as it flies
Lives in Eternity's sunrise.
                              —William Blake

She closed her eyes for a few moments, feeling
again the sun on her brow. The moment was
delicious, one to be savoured.
                              —Alexander McCall Smith

Savoring—that delicious word—is a way of experiencing the world most vividly and beautifully. It is a kind of art, too, for savoring doesn't just happen; it needs an open and hospitable soul, a large soul with an expansive openness to awe, and a willingness to practice it daily. What does it mean to practice the art of savoring? We might call it "deep awareness" or "capturing the moment," or as Blake says, "kissing the joy as it flies." We often think that such lofty notions must be the sole territory of the contemplative, the painter, the photographer, and the poet. But savoring is really a universal art, something everyone can practice. I know its power on a personal level, but I cannot write about it without including a kaleidoscope of metaphors.

Melting into the Moment
    When I think of the word "savor," what first comes to mind is fine chocolate, the rich, dark chocolate that melts slowly in the mouth, the kind of chocolate that warrants perfect concentration and stillness of body—and certainly the closing of eyes. It's as if the taste starts in

the mouth, like any other food, but the surprise is too startling, too overwhelming, to be held by the taste buds alone, so the dark joy moves along like an overflowing river into the tributaries of body. But savoring is not confined to taste. A moment of savoring may occur while basking cat-like in a shaft of warm sunshine on a wintery day, or gazing up at a flock of pelicans overhead, or listening to Mozart. We want the moment not simply to pass, but to melt—to melt slowly. Savoring is a kind of melting into the moment and letting the moment melt into us.

Such moments can transform a person's life, but they are never solely intellectual. In the act of savoring, all the senses wake up and the world becomes vivid and delicious. For Isabel Dalhousie, the Edinburgh philosopher in Alexander McCall Smith's lovely novel series, such a moment changes everything. She is standing in an Edinburgh gallery courtyard when she realizes that the man she loves reciprocates in full measure. She is loved, truly loved. She discovers by accident a secret painting he has bought for her, and the joy of it stops time. "It was a moment," writes the Scottish novelist, "of realisation, of understanding, and it took place against a background of sun and geraniums and the pure voice of a bird."[11]

Kissing the Joy

We know that the savored moment is temporary, fleeting: a moment of "perpetual perishing" as Whitehead would say. But it is that very ephemeral quality of the moment which creates the heightened awareness of joy. We try to slow down the moment, to stretch it out, to capture it in its entirety.

Savoring is a form of mindfulness; it is gratitude, too. When gratitude and mindfulness unite in spontaneous union, something beautiful begins to quake inside of us, and we cannot let such a moment pass like any other; no, it is a moment that must be noted and cherished before it wings its way toward the rebirth of eternally new moments. And even then, we yearn after it with a desire to protect it, keep it, own it. But the moment cannot be held any longer than we can hold a quivering bird in our hand. This is simply the way of things; this is the process of Eternal Flow.

Gathering Exquisite Moments

But we want things to last, don't we? Poignancy hovers around beauty like a nimbus, for the most beautiful things in life are not things at all, but moments in time—moments that we know will flow on. While the raw moment flows on into a new concrescence, we can nevertheless gather the exquisite moments like flowers and place them in the rose bowl of our memories.

Rose bowls were popular in Victorian times. Roses were cut at the height of their beauty, just before they perished, to float about in an enormous bowl—a thing of beauty in itself, usually silver or china or glass—and placed in the entry way of the house. The floating roses and other delicate flowers set the tone for the home: to remind the household of the fleeting quality of all things precious, and of the fragility of each person who inhabits the home—and that we need to be kind.

The Great Paradox

So we gather up our moments, the ones most exquisite, and let them float about inside us as we savor their color, scent, and texture. Even though the memory is not the same as the moment itself—even memory is a new moment—we can store up an entire bowl of exquisite memory moments that we can enjoy later. But what if our memory fails, as it so often does? Process theology tells us that if we forget, God still remembers. Our moments are saved in God's memory, in God's own heart. The moments we savor are paradoxically fleeting and eternal in the same divine breath. They are gone, yes, but not lost. Whitehead describes God's nature as "tender care that nothing be lost."[12]

So if we think that our moments with Mozart might be useless to anyone or anything beyond ourselves, we need to think again. Savoring adds to the joy of God for all eternity. And that moment savored not only contributes to God's joy, but to the joy of the entire cosmos. When we kiss the joy with mindful gratitude, we unleash fresh possibilities for the next sunrise. It is inevitable; joy is like that: it spills over into eternity.

Exquisite Empathy

Gathering up exquisite moments—the art of savoring—is a worthy purpose for each day. We can easily practice this art when the confluence of events intermingles with our own mindfulness and gratitude, creating intensely harmonious moments.

But if we want to go deeper still, we need to learn how to savor when things go badly, too—when the warmth and chocolate and pelicans are gone, or when loved ones fail us and our insecurities rise up to mock us. This is life, too. On those dark days, when nothing seems worth salvaging, we can still practice the art of savoring, for there is something even more satisfying that deserves our mindfulness and gratitude: we can savor the One who savors us.

If we can learn to see not just the lack of roses in our bowl, but the bowl itself—the Encircling One—we will touch the ultimate joy, the Ultimate itself. In process theology, we name the Encircling One, God. Whitehead says, "God is the great companion—the fellow sufferer who understands."[13] Words to savor, are they not?

S-I-Z-I-N-G Up

Becoming wide and beautiful and spacious souls begins when we embrace the simple fact that we are loved, truly loved—perhaps not by everyone we know, but always and eternally by the Encircling One. Savoring is a way of touching this beauty and participating in the beauty of God. So, no matter what happens, we can let this thought melt into us: God holds us in exquisite empathy, and reminds us that life is eternally blooming with fresh possibilities.

The Beauty of Imperfection

There is no perfection, only beautiful versions of brokenness.
—Shannon L. Alder

Typos are the bane of my existence. Maybe I'm just a singularly neurotic writer, but I doubt that I'm alone in this. Trying to rid a manuscript of typos is like guerrilla warfare in the jungle. The brutality never ends—never. Just when you start to feel safe, the misplaced comma, the missing quotation mark, the glaring absence of a preposition, or worst of all, the misspelled word will ambush you. Typos are sinister; they taunt and mock and jeer for the sport of it—it's what they do. It's their *raison d'etre.* That's why writers have someone else proof their work, but even then, some particularly devious typos sneak by the editor into publication, like stowaways on a ship waiting with evil relish to emerge, brazenly, just after the boat sails.

Would I have it any other way? Would it be better to half-heartedly glance over my work and pronounce it "good enough"? Of course not. I think it's good to struggle with something you love—to do some serious suffering, even while knowing that perfection is elusive. Striving for perfection has its moments—think of great pianists or Olympic athletes—and it can even save lives. I fervently hope that people who dismantle bombs are perfectionists, obsessively so, as well as doctors who perform delicate surgery. And heaven help us if our dentists declare a botched root canal, "good enough."

We need to strive for excellence, of course we do.

But we need to be wary of perfectionism, for as we climb that steep mountain on our way to our ideal, we might just lose our footing and go crashing down in a heap. Perfectionism has a dark and dangerous side.

Perfectionism: The Dark Side

Perfectionism, a fairly innocuous word, can in fact make us miserable and neurotic and play heinous tricks on our psyche. It can make us sick. Perfectionism is a dangerous game and, if not watched carefully, can turn tragic. For example, women are inundated from an early age with magazine ads showing gaunt, curveless bodies as if they are the "ideal." Anything outside the perimeters of that ultra-thin, half-emaciated ideal is to be stamped INFERIOR, and thus most of us go around feeling quite dissatisfied with—or even ashamed of—our bodies. Thanks to the Tyranny of Thin, eating disorders continue to take their toll on—even kill—bright, talented young women.

Remember Karen Carpenter. Listen to her voice and weep for all that was lost. She died of complications from anorexia nervosa at age 32, a complex illness, but one in which a driving force is perfectionism-gone-mad. And for the anorexic, perfectionism does not stop with body image, but infiltrates the whole personality. One's entire life-orientation becomes hostage to elusive ideals of perfection.

On the socio-political level, radical ideologues strive, sometimes violently, for their version of the perfect political system or perfect religion. Worse still—maybe worst of all—are those who believe in an ideal skin color or "race." History breaks our hearts with its testimony of such madness.

Granted, these are extreme examples, but even in our everyday lives we are besieged by this vague, unspoken notion that there are "ideals" out there that we have to live up to, or else we are simply inferior beings that might as well be wiped off the page like dangling modifiers. We feel we need the perfect house, the perfect spouse, the perfect job, the perfect nose—even perfect happiness.

Tracking Down the Source . . .

Chasing after elusive ideals: Where does this compulsion come from? Who can we blame for the tormenting power of perfectionism to blight our peace of mind? Our parents? Our culture? Our "superegos"? Maybe. But in this essay, I'm going to blame Plato. Yes, Plato. He was the philosopher who came up with the whole idea of perfection in the first place. Of course, Plato pretty much laid the foundations for Western Civilization, so it's best not to be too hard on him. Can you imagine a world without, say, *The Republic*? Socrates himself? Never. Plato taught us through Socrates how to think critically, how to examine our lives. Plato had his moments. Yet, there is a downside to the great philosopher. Yes, it's true—and I say this with relish: Plato was NOT PERFECT.

Plato's Flaw

Truth is, Plato left to his own devices can cause a great deal of mischief. He believed that every imperfect thing has a perfect ideal in some heavenly realm—and that only those perfect "forms" are truly, truly real. Everything else—actual people, trees, and monkeys are mere shadows of their perfect counterpart ideals. It's as if there are perfect Greek statues lined up in the heavens: perfect body, perfect tree, perfect monkey—all looking down on us in judgment.

And the more divergent something is from the perfect ideal, the less value it has. You can see the disturbing moral implications piling up here. Rabbi Bradley Shavit Artson explains this particularly well in his book *God of Becoming and Relationship: The Dynamic Nature of Process Theology* where he takes on Plato's perfect forms. He says, "A view that elevates the ideal is profoundly mistrustful of any individuality, of people being stubbornly not the ideal, of being irreducibly unique and different. It is also important to point out that if the ideal is perfect and if the physical is denigrated, then how much more so are people who are physically disabled or socially degraded: how inferior are they!"[14] Rabbi Artson gives a compelling argument for both process theology and Jewish thought as remedies for this huge flaw in Plato.

Thinking of Jesus may be another remedy for Plato's obsession with abstract perfectionism and ideal forms. Jesus much preferred real, earthy, imperfect people—sinners, tax collectors, and the "least of these"— to the "perfect" Pharisees. Perfect people don't have the capacity for love like imperfect people. Jesus knew that; he knew that only love is the answer to the mystery of life—not perfection.

The Consolation of *Wabi-Sabi*

Yet another remedy for getting Mr. Perfect, aka Plato, off our backs comes from Japan. The Japanese do not revere Plato like we Westerners do. Thank goodness. When the tyranny of perfectionism hits, we can turn to the Japanese notion of *wabi-sabi* for consolation. What is *wabi-sabi*? To me it is a bed of flowers in which to rest after typos have taken their exhausting, demoralizing toll on the spirit. *Wabi-sabi* is a Japanese aesthetic, a view of beauty that actually embraces imperfection.

Richard Powell, in his book *Wabi Sabi Simple,* explains that *wabi-sabi* "nurtures all that is authentic by acknowledging three simple realities: nothing lasts, nothing is finished, and nothing is perfect."[15] This is a Buddhist way of thinking, and the Japanese prefer this as a standard for beauty rather than Plato's ideal forms. In a spiritual sense, *wabi-sabi* says to us: Perfectionists, step aside! Bring in the rustic tea pot, chipped and scarred with use; the fallen leaf, brown and withered; the old woman, wrinkled and full of history and stories. All these are beautiful, my friends, if only you could see.

As a process thinker, I am drawn to *wabi-sabi*. Here in Ecuador, I have recently created a *wabi-sabi* rock garden—a simple, earthy affair of collected rocks washed in by the tide, set in the form of a spiral so it can go on and on as I find more rocks. Not only is it forever unfinished, it is also filled with diverse, rough, oddly shaped rocks of various colors and sizes—all of which somehow create a more intense harmony. This is a process view of beauty: the beauty is in the differences, like the different notes of a chord of music, each note with its own integrity—together spilling out into the air in clusters of intense harmony that further the Creative Advance of the universe.

Widening Circles

"I live my life in widening circles," says the poet Rilke. In the spirit of Rilke, my *wabi-sabi* garden is designed in an open-ended spiral, so it will grow in size to make room for more rocks. It is a rock garden in process—a widening beauty—an unfinished becoming rather than a static being. So it is with our very souls; they are not static "things." We are not perfect, self-enclosed billiard balls bumping up against each other. We are created out of our relatedness to one another—and to the past and possible future. We are hurt by our relationships and we are healed by our relationships. And we are forever free to choose a more healing path, a more beautiful path than the one we are on.

Our souls or psyches constantly erupt into fresh becomings and can, despite the pressure of the past, re-imagine the world in widening circles. The beautiful soul, the wide soul—or what I like to call the Fat Soul—does not subscribe to the narrow ideals thrust upon it by the Tyranny of Thin mentality. The Fat Soul is one that, for the sake of love and beauty and intensity of feeling, expands to include the so-called imperfect, the not-quite-right, and the sweet but sad melancholy of "perpetual perishing."

And So, Dear Plato . . .

Thus, beauty in terms of process thought and *wabi-sabi* bears scant resemblance to the Platonic ideals of abstract perfection to which we must aspire or be counted inferior. We "subversives" who stand up against the Tyranny of Thin and all the trouble perfectionism has wrought in the world, choose instead to fatten our vision, our psyches, our souls. Rather than hold ourselves up to a static, abstract perfection, we choose to embrace the warts-and-all diversity and contrasts in the real world of fresh becomings. We choose to love our unfinished selves, our bodies, our work, our relationships—all in their natural "imperfections" and unique differences. We throw out our scales and give ourselves over to a worldview with wide hips—one that can make room for all the variegated colors and shapes and striking contrasts that make life beautiful.

And so, dear Plato, father of Western Civilization, I apologize for being so hard on you. You are part of us, we Westerners, religious and secular alike, who have been raised on your static ideas of perfection. We will not abandon you. You have given us so much. After all, Whitehead said that the whole tradition of Western philosophy is a series of footnotes to you.[16] You are simply unfinished and imperfect like the rest of us. But cheer up, Plato. Even as we declare you to be flawed as an ancient Greek statue missing an arm, in the spirit of process and *wabi-sabi*, we also pronounce you *beautiful*.

—Personal Postscript—

There is a flaw in the above essay, and it has nothing to do with typos. After writing and re-writing and writing again, I couldn't quite get a handle on the problem. It was too deep and elusive—and subconsciously troubling. Something was wrong. In frustration, I played an old album by Karen Carpenter and I suddenly realized the problem with a jolt. Her beautiful, rich, contralto voice was the very lure I needed to say something I never dreamed of saying out-loud in public—and certainly never in writing! But her voice from "long ago and oh, so far away" insisted that what I needed to add, if I was to be true to the words above, is this: I am not merely a distant observer. I am a survivor of anorexia nervosa.

In the late 1970s (in my early-twenties), I developed the disease even while Karen Carpenter was losing her battle. She was an icon for me, someone I adored, a fellow musician. She was perfect. I wanted to be. She died and I lived. It could have been me, as we weighed exactly the same: 91 lbs. And yet, even in that emaciated state, I felt that if I just lost another pound or two, I would be perfect. It took an intervention and a stern doctor's warning that I had to choose life or die. I chose life. I was lucky to get the help I needed, but it was a long, long road to recovery. My weight eventually became normal, but I learned that you don't ever quite shake off the demons. They are always there, lurking in the shadows, but the difference is that they lose their power over your life.

Although there are many new theories about the disease, including many biological and genetic factors that doctors were not aware of in the 1970s, perfectionism and the need for control over one's life, two central features of the illness, are not only treatable but can also be transformed. I am living proof. Treatment is one thing, but transformation takes years. I'm not sure that I would have made it even to age thirty-two, the age Karen Carpenter's heart gave out, if I had not learned how to slowly transform my entire worldview.

Through the years, process thought—especially process theology—helped expand my narrow, severe, impoverished view of myself, God, and the world into a lovely, widening landscape of beauty, love, and letting go. The psychological effect of process theology helped me slowly regain my health and, eventually, flourish. Yet when, as a professional minister and teacher, I encountered anorexic girls, I related to them only as an objective professional, keeping my own "imperfect" past to myself. But now I am too old and life is too short for such distance and pretense. At least that's what Karen Carpenter was telling me with her voice from somewhere in heaven.

I realize now that my essay was not so much imperfect as it was too perfect. It lacked the embodiment of my own imperfect authenticity—a personal story that might help someone who is suffering. Now, with this added postscript, the essay feels authentic, *wabi-sabi*—an imperfect offering.

S-I-Z-I-N-G Up

We starve our souls (and sometimes even our bodies) in the elusive quest for perfection. We contract rather than expand when we demand perfection from ourselves. It all goes back to that lurking fear that we are "not good enough." In order to grow our souls into something beautiful, we must create a space in our souls for imperfection, even for those disquieting voices that taunt us with our inadequacies. This place inside our soul will need to be a spacious room with plenty of soft cushions. Perhaps you can imagine a softly lit room in your soul that is inhabited by a rocking chair. In that chair sits your best self, your divinely drenched self, which is the seat of unconditional love. Sitting on your lap is your wounded inner child that cries out, "I'm a total failure! I'm not good enough!" If you rock this baby long enough and speak to that sense of failure with loving words, then nothing can destroy you. You will soon learn to take yourself less seriously, accept yourself as you are— even your neurotic quest for perfection—and rebound quickly. We have come a long way toward Fat Soulhood when this truth finally takes hold of us.

Help!
I'm an Introvert
in an Extrovert World

Introversion—along with its cousins sensitivity, seriousness, and shyness—is now a second-class personality trait, somewhere between a disappointment and a pathology. Introverts living under the Extrovert Ideal are like women in a man's world, discounted because of a trait that goes to the core of who they are.

—Susan Cain

Sometimes I wonder what it would be like to be an extrovert—yes, to be comfortable in crowds, to speak extemporaneously with easy charisma. To be the life of the party! To not only *type* an exclamation mark at the end of a sentence that you hope conveys enthusiasm and ultra-sincerity, but to *live* those exclamation marks! To live double exclamation marks!! (If the very sight of all these exclamation marks exhausts you—maybe even repels you—you are probably an introvert like me.)

Oh, but I do love extroverts. I love to listen to their stories; I am drawn by their charisma; I stand in awe at their ability to draw energy from being with other people. To live the life of "action." To speak fast. To multitask. Wow. I do admire them. But I no longer feel the need to be like them. And more importantly, I no longer believe that I have a second-class personality. Part of this enlightenment is due to the wisdom of age and part of it is due to Susan Cain and her book *Quiet: The Power of Introverts in a World that Won't Stop Talking.*[17]

The Culture of Personality

Cain explains how, beginning in the early twentieth century, the Culture of Personality replaced the nineteenth-century ideal of the Culture of Character. American culture moved away from values like citizenship, duty, honor, morals, manners, and integrity, and now preferred people who were: magnetic, fascinating, stunning, attractive, glowing, dominant, forceful, energetic (i.e., the exclamation mark people!). While the Culture of Character could be embodied by extroverts and introverts alike, the Cultural of Personality elevates qualities that lie primarily in the realm of the extrovert. For the rest of us, they spell H-E-L-L.

Best-selling author of his day Orison Swett Marden, who in 1899 wrote *Character: The Grandest Thing,* later captured the dynamic new vision of the Culture of Personality, and in 1921 wrote another best-seller called *Masterful Personality.*   This means that American culture slowly began to idealize extroverts as the upper class of personalities, relegating introverts to steerage.   The Dale Carnegies of this world became aligned with what Cain calls "the Extrovert Ideal," and by the 1950s and 60s, this cultural philosophy was already canonized by most of our social institutions.

Cain explains how, beginning in the 1950s, parents were told to watch out for the shy "maladjusted" child. Yes, we who shunned pep rallies were maladjusted. My own dear mother, a modern 1950s and 60s parent, was naturally influenced by this cultural warning about shy children.   My mind whips back to 1969 when she encouraged me to try out for Ninth Grade Cheerleader. Nothing could have been more mortifying for a shy introvert. Mercifully, I didn't make the cut—but I tried out because I was told it would make me more "outgoing," and everyone wanted to be "outgoing." It was simply a cultural given.

Naturally, as a teen growing up in the blooming days of the Culture of Personality, choosing to read the Bronte sisters in my room rather than go out with friends was worrisome. I was pegged by adults as one of those unfortunate children who suffered from the "inferiority complex." That was what every parent worried about: the inferiority complex, i.e., the shy child.

As far as boys went, my mom was especially worried. If I couldn't be a cheerleader, could I not, at the very least, set my sights on a football player? But around football players I was hopelessly shy. And uninterested. I didn't particularly like football. Did that matter? No. I needed to be—not to put too fine a point on it—more OUTGOING.

Oh, To Be Fascinating!

About the same time I failed to make cheerleader, my mother presented me with a book called *Fascinating Womanhood* by Helen Andelin (1963). It was The Bible for all young women coming of age in the Culture of Personality. I was baffled by the book back then, but now it makes perfect sense. Susan Cain explains that the forceful, "masterful personality" was primarily meant for business men, "but women were urged to work on a mysterious quality called 'fascination.'"[18] It remained a mysterious quality to me.

One night I came home from a party early (as usual) to be confronted by an anxious mother. She sat me down. We talked about a particular boy. I explained that I had his attention, but couldn't think of anything to say to him. She looked worried and said, "So, you just sat there and said nothing? Like a bump on a log?" Great, I thought. Now I'm a bump on a log. That's about as far from fascinating as you can get.

So I began to think that, yes, I must have an inferiority complex. I am unfascinating. I am flawed to the core. Who could save me? Was I doomed to be a bump on a log forever?

Religion.   Maybe that would save me.   It was supposed to save people.   And it did.   I found great comfort in my youth group, and even though it was very social, it still allowed me to go off alone on retreats and read the Bible and think about things.   There I was considered "spiritual" rather than "maladjusted," clearly an improvement.   And the boys at church were more approachable, too, at least some of them.   Susan Cain says that introverts, particularly sensitive introverts, are often drawn to religion and philosophy.   Was I not a textbook case?

Church, back then, was not as extrovert as it is today.   I didn't have to go around hugging everyone and clapping and greeting my neighbors in the pew each Sunday.   I could listen and think and dream and pray. That was paradise, albeit, short-lived.   After Sunday's respite into quietness, it was Monday again, and back to the social pressures of school, where the Pep Club alone forced me to become a philosopher, an existentialist, a "Hell is other people" sort of young thinker (I've always had a soft spot for Sartre).

Tonic for the Shy?

I Love Lucy re-runs were my favorite after school activity.   But alas, even television was infiltrated by the Extrovert Ideal.   Remember Lucy's "Vitameatavegamin" commercial?   This tonic not only promised to cure those who were "tired, run-down, and listless," but also made you socially courageous.   Yes, it could make you popular! She spooned out a dose while saying into the camera, "Are you unpopular?   Do you poop out at parties?"   All you needed, of course, was Vitameatavegamin.   And, as she kept spooning the alcohol-laden syrup into her mouth, it became slurred into: "Are you unpoopular?   Do you pop out at parties?"   Who can forget that?

I still love Lucy (one of my favorite all-time extroverts), but do we really need a tonic made with 23% alcohol to cure our natural-born tendencies to read *Jane Eyre* in our room rather than jump and scream at pep rallies? And, in an updated version of Vitameatavegamin, do we really need those high-priced drugs that promise to cure our "social anxiety"?

As Cain points out, we have not gotten past the Culture of Personality. In fact, it's worse—much worse. We're like the Culture of Personality on steroids. Today, it's hard to find a job where you don't have to be or *pretend* to be an extrovert. The Culture of Personality is everywhere: business schools, churches, educational philosophies, and politics—particularly politics. You can't escape the tentacles of the Extrovert Ideal. (*Fascinating Womanhood* is in its sixth edition.)

The Shy Philosopher

No wonder I'm a Whiteheadian. Alfred North Whitehead (1861-1947) was not only a brilliant mathematician and philosopher, but also a famously shy introvert, according to Jerome Kagan in *Galen's Prophecy: Temperament in Human Nature*. As Cain points out, in Kagan's Harvard studies with children, he compares one thoughtful, shy child named Tom, who wants to be a scientist, to T. S. Eliot and Whitehead, both of whom were also shy as children, and so grew up to choose the "life of the mind."[19]

I find comfort here. For here we see that shy children, if not forced to be "outgoing" by well-meaning parents and teachers, can grow up be quite bold in their own introverted way. Whitehead wrote *Process and Reality* at Harvard just as the Culture of Personality was picking up steam. But he evidently did not pay attention to the Zeitgeist. Rather than seek popularity, Whitehead quietly and persistently forged a bold new path in philosophy—abolishing Cartesian dualism and ushering in a "philosophy of organism" for the interconnected quantum world in which we now live. This philosophy cut against the grain of the more popular trend of analytic philosophy of the time. Pretty darned bold for a quiet man.

Spirituality for the Shy

As a spiritual person, what I like best about the famously introverted Whitehead, is that he presents a view of God that does not fit into the Culture of Personality. No wonder process theology is a minority view, for Whitehead's God is simply not "outgoing" enough. No Master of the Universe here! Rather than having a "masterful personality," his God "dwells in the tender elements in the world, which slowly and in quietness operate by love."[20] I think this view of God and the world brings out the more noble aspects of religious thought.

What if Whitehead had not been born in nineteenth-century Britain? What if he had been brought up in the Culture of Personality in America? What if his mother had given him Vitameatavegamin or some other magical tonic to cure him of living too much in his head? What if his mother had forced him to take a Dale Carnegie course at the YMCA so he could better "win friends and influence people"?

Good Heavens! Just try to imagine a world without introverts: A universe devoid of many of our greatest philosophers and scientists and religious thinkers and writers and poets and humanitarians; a world without van Gogh, Chopin, Rosa Parks, Eleanor Roosevelt, Gandhi—it doesn't bear thinking about.

Inspiration from an Extrovert

Those of us who are introverts need to unite and reclaim our self-esteem, our sense of purpose in the world, equal in every way to our more fascinating friends. I think our extrovert friends would join us in our cause, because many of them, too, question the dubious morality of the Culture of Personality, which blithely—while we weren't looking—usurped the Culture of Character. Take one of the most famous extroverts in recent history, Martin Luther King, Jr. He used his natural charisma, not for charisma's sake, not for the sake of the Culture of Personality, but for this one thing:

that all children "will one day live in a nation where they will not be judged by the color of their skin, but by *the content of their character.*"

Just thinking of MLK gives me courage. Yes, it's time for introverts to unite and make our stand. We need to tell the world that we refuse to be treated as second-class personalities! (Maybe we could meet in the library.)

S-I-Z-I-N-G Up

Fat Soul is, thankfully, not just for introverts. (I would be lost without my extrovert friends, and much impoverished in spirit.)   But if you are an introvert, embrace it. Expand in your own quiet way. If you are an extrovert, embrace that, too.   And then let's stretch toward each other—even if we have to move outside our comfort zone from time to time for the sake of something larger. For the truth is, we need each other to make a more beautiful, soulful world.

Replanting Yourself in Beauty

Let everything happen to you: beauty and terror.
Just keep going. No feeling is final.
                              —Rainer Maria Rilke

Lying awake at 3:00 a.m. on a board covered with a thin mattress, I ache from my neck to my toes. I am in a strange land and I cannot sleep. Something vital is missing, something from my homeland, my past, and I cannot go back and get it. My "self" as I know her is somewhere back there, while my body lies here: I am stretched out on this painful reality.

All the invisible layers of security and comfort that have secretly supported me from the day of my birth suddenly become visible and real at the very moment of their departure. The void is dark and hard and hurting. This is how terror feels.

I imagine this is how it must feel when you lose a spouse or a best friend, or even a job. But I have not lost anything really, except a home, a place, a people, a language, and a feeling of safety and security. So yes, I have to face it: I feel like my life has been pulled out from beneath me. I must be experiencing the throes of culture shock: the grief, the loss, the terror of being an alien in a strange land.

So here I am, in Ecuador, lying wide-eyed in the long equatorial night of darkness, on a bed of torture, a rack really, in a cheap hostel (feeling more like its homonym "hostile") in the cold, rainy city of Quito. I am waiting for sunrise, for at least that, for light, and possibly some toast and juice. Later, my husband and I will make yet another frustrating attempt at securing our residency visas. With so many attempts and always an obstacle, we feel like Sisyphus, and we are tired of the effort.

I look over at my husband, who is sleeping annoyingly sound while I struggle over not only the sanity of the whole enterprise of uprooting and moving to South America, but my ability to withstand such an uprooting. I had been like a mature tree—even blooming on occasion —but now I am lost to the familiar, only to be replanted in the soil of the terrifying unknown. "Bloom where you are planted," the proverb goes. But the transplant is not taking hold. I am a rootless tree.

The Year of Terror and Beauty

That night on the "rack" in Quito was just the beginning of a difficult year punctuated by many sleepless nights. Of course we were we dealing with psychic vicissitudes of culture shock, which had anticipated; but we were not prepared for our adventure to spin suddenly into misadventure.

We did get our residency visas, and thought that would be the end of it, the end of the difficulties in our new land. So we set out with great enthusiasm to fulfill our dream, to build our home—plans that my husband had personally designed—so we could finally root ourselves in our new world. But that dream was quickly derailed in a building scam, resulting in the loss of tens of thousands of dollars we could ill afford to lose. Our home building came to a standstill for months, as did our hearts. We were in a foreign country with no home and not enough money to build one, and we could not go back where we came from. Not long after this shock, we were taking a walk to discuss what to do next when we were mugged at knife-point and gunpoint. After that, we lost all sense of security in our new world. By the end of the year, we were two adventurers bedraggled by events and actions completely outside of our control.

But Ecuador is not to be blamed. Ecuador is a dazzlingly beautiful country with mostly generous people and so much to offer the rest of the world. But this larger picture was not enough to keep terror at bay.

But larger questions did help. I had to go beyond my personal pain to ask the bigger question: How can my philosophy help when change and loss feel utterly overwhelming, when fear paralyzes, when one's whole sense of security is undermined? I realized that such an existential crisis as mine—this painful Questioning of Everything—does not only wreck the sleep of someone moving to another country; it lies in wait at 3:00 a.m. for any adventurer who dares to love, to risk, to live vividly, to roam beyond the boundaries of the familiar.

"The Adventure of the Universe starts with a dream and reaps tragic beauty."[21] Whitehead's famous quote about the nature of God and the world, which I had carried in the back of my mind to Ecuador, became a source of healing for me that first year. This bit of theology, set in poetry, rooted me to the earth over and over again. It is just this way: If we adventurers are to follow the lure of the Divine Adventurer, then our dreams, too, will inevitably collide with reality—even at times, with terror and evil. But that's not the whole of it. That's not the end. Beauty, the goal of the Adventurer, is also the guide. How, Beauty asks of us, can we weave this tragic thread into the whole of it with wisdom and skill and an artist's eye? Or, in this case, how can we use the very depth and darkness of the pain to plant new roots and nourish them in a new land?

Replanting Myself in Beauty

With Beauty's questions in mind, I went to work to establish very practical steps, daily habits and rituals that would enable me to tap into the rich, fertile soil deep down inside me. What I needed was to slowly and patiently replant myself in Beauty. Looking back now, I can identify five habits of Beauty.

Natural Beauty: On my daily beach walks at low tide I would commune with the graceful pelicans and the white egrets and the skittering sand crabs, while allowing the natural rhythms of the sea to embrace me in the larger Flow of things. I learned firsthand what Rachel Carson believed, that "Those who dwell . . . among the beauties and mysteries of the earth are never alone or weary of life."[22]

The Arts and Creativity: I took several minutes each day to listen on my iPod to the calming, balancing keyboard works of J. S. Bach. Besides music, I needed creative mental work, so I carved out time to write, even if it was only a journal entry.

Meditation: Mindfulness meditation enabled me to hold everything gently—even my terror and rage—like a parent caring for child. Meditation, even in tiny increments, trains us not to grasp too hard or demand too much; it also teaches us not to push away our fears. It teaches us to open wide to the moving, undulating, "never final" universe which sustains us.

Community: "Only connect" is the continuing refrain of E. M. Forster's novel, *Howard's End*, which I read and re-read on my Kindle during my year of terror. My connection to nature is easy, but when it comes to people I tend to be an introvert. Nevertheless, my husband and I both reached out to find community support with other expats from North America. And we have extended that sense of community to the Ecuadorians around us, despite the language difficulties. This sense of ever-widening circles of community and cultural enrichment has given us a sense of belonging in our new world.

Beautiful Thinking: Here is where our philosophy of life, our meaning-making comes into play. Our favorite books such as sacred texts, theology, philosophy, psychology, *Jesus, Jazz, and Buddhism* essays, novels, and poetry help feed the mind with thoughts that create harmony of mind and soul. Journaling helps, too. I found a form of cognitive therapy called REBT particularly useful in my journaling as I rooted out flaws in my thinking. I also memorized bits of Rilke's poetry, verses from the Bible, and many calming

affirmations.   The affirmation-oriented writings of
process theologian Bruce Epperly have been particularly
helpful. (Below is the working-out of my own needed
affirmation on the path to beauty.)

Letting Go, Trusting, Choosing Beauty

Feeling "out of control" is a major stressor—
especially, I have found, in a foreign country.   For
example, in Latin America things never happen when
they are supposed to; they just happen when they
happen. When someone says that something will happen
mañana, it is does not mean "tomorrow." It means "not
today." Latin America humbles those who think they can
organize their lives with schedules and date books. All
this is frustrating, and one feels constantly "out of
control."

Learning to let go of the need to control is vital.
But of course, on a metaphysical level, nothing really is
fully within our control to start with. We are never, at
any time, omnipotent; nor are we ever completely
powerless. So we can learn to accept this basic relational
fact by letting go of our demands on life, others, and
ourselves. We can desire that things go well, but we
cannot demand it. We have power, but our power is
relational and limited. So, when we are overwhelmed by
events outside our immediate influence—when we feel
angry and helpless and afraid—we must first learn to
release our demands on life, on others, and on ourselves.
Demands do not work in a relational universe, and
certainly not in Latin America.

For those of us who are process-oriented, we can
also trust in our understanding of a loving, suffering,
creative God, who feels our terror in all of its intensity
and offers transformative possibilities. Here is my own
three-step affirmation that I relied on during that difficult
first year, and still recite today when facing frustration,
fear, and helplessness:

I let go of the demands I place on life, others, and myself.
I trust in God's creative transformation and healing.
I choose the path of Beauty.

Improvisation

By "the path of Beauty" I mean that we need to choose the most beautiful response for this particular moment, e.g., forgiveness, creative problem solving, courageous action, listening, prayer, stillness. What choice is right for the situation at hand? This is where maturity and wisdom and sensitivity to the "divine lure" from the Adventurer of the universe come into play. It is our moment of improvisation.

As for my husband and me, we are back to building our home—a simpler home than the one we started out building, but a far more interesting one, with improvised elements from the eye of an artistic architect. Our little *casa*-in-the-making is now, like the lives of its owners, becoming what it can be for this creative moment. Next year, we may add-on or revise, or maybe not. We are learning to let our dreams unfold in the creative vortex of life-as-it-is instead of life-as-we-demand-it-to-be. Beauty is there always, re-working, re-creating, re-envisioning. This is what a process vision of the world gives us: it gives us open-endedness; it gives us hope.

So then, as Rilke says, we need to feel it all: the whole of it, the beauty and the terror. This does not mean we are passive pawns in a fatalistic universe. On the contrary, we have the power of improvisation in this universe of Flow where "no feeling is final." We can let go, we can trust, we can walk the path of Beauty. This is how we "keep going." But we do not walk alone. With the companionship of divine Beauty always re-creating out of chaos and pain, we can finally relax and let our roots spread deeply and peacefully into the welcoming earth, wherever we happen to be.

S-I-Z-I-N-G Up

Widening out in the midst of fear is one of the most challenging of our soul-stretching efforts. We want the beauty of spaciousness, yes, but beauty is hard, for it demands much of us. It is easier to shrink back, contract our souls, and pull the covers over our heads. We may need to go deep before we can go wide. We need roots in order to expand and feel calm and strong and solid; like a tree, we would simply topple over without deep, wide, well-nourished roots. Family, friends, community, art, nature, animals, faith, love—all these forms of beauty can create large and luminous souls and banish fear from our lives. Take time to explore your own roots—or lack thereof—and re-imagine how you might replant yourself in beauty.

Fat Soul, Happy Soul

Being able to enjoy happiness doesn't require that we have zero suffering. In fact, the art of happiness is also the art of suffering well.
—Thich Nhat Hanh

"Happiness." That word, that singular sound made up of three scintillating syllables, entices us every time we hear it or read it or think it. Even if we are sad or cynical or, even worse, confirmed happiness atheists, we still yearn for it, don't we? Are we to pursue happiness for ourselves? Is that selfish? Delusional? It can be. But I believe there is something noble—even beautiful—in the pursuit, especially for Fat Souls—those working to expand their souls for the sake of beauty.

For a Fat Soul is a beautiful soul, a resilient soul, a never-quite-full soul because it continually indulges in delicious things like fresh ideas, empathy, curiosity, listening, gratitude, and generosity of spirit. These are soul-stretching words, fat words, words that balloon out from our personal space and connect us to the world, to many worlds—big and small and far away worlds. They connect us to the deepness and wideness of life itself. This is what I call Big Happiness.

Making Room for a Little Irony

Big Happiness outweighs old notions of happiness, i.e., purely individualistic and hedonistic. Big Happiness cannot exist in a vacuum, by and for itself alone. It is connected to every other person on the earth, to every creature, to the very molecules that make up the planet and the stars.

But embracing this fact—yes, the scientific fact—that *we are connected* has a price. Big Happiness means that we have to invite in unhappiness, too, and care for it. If that sounds ironic or a total paradox, then you've got the notion correct. For a soul that excludes or denies the darkness is a very shallow soul, indeed, and will have to settle for the barest and most artificial forms of happiness. That soul will never find meaning; it will never know Big Happiness. For a soul that has not been shattered by loss or has never agonized over the inherent difficulties of a meaningful relationship or experienced the poignancy of passing beauty—that is a soul bereft and impoverished.

So, too, Fat Souls know the meaning of out-and-out rage when witnessing racism or animal suffering or the planet's ongoing desecration due to greed. When we make room for even these unhappy feelings, we can somehow bear them and love them into transformation, sometimes through healing action. We can create—or co-create with God—something fresh and soul-expanding and ultimately meaningful with our anger and despair.

Another note of subtle irony about the Fat Soul is this: despite its largesse, it has boundaries—integrity, if you will. For a Fat Soul is not a chaotic free-for-all, but a soul in search of intense harmony. So you don't embrace everything indiscriminately; sometimes you have to say no to a bad idea, a manipulative person, or anything that will ultimately diminish rather than expand the soul. But even in that Big Fat NO! you can do it with kindness; not a violent pushing away, but a letting go, a gentle release of that which one knows will ultimately impoverish and shrink the soul. This means that you have to apply the same generosity of spirit that you offer others to your own soul—taking care of yourself, acknowledging your own pain, and treating yourself with daily helpings of what Buddhists call lovingkindness. Without this ability to indulge in lovingkindness towards yourself, happiness will elude you, and everyone around you will be a little less happy, too.

A Deliciously Fattening Two-Layer Exercise

Meditating on this idea, I envisioned a little mental exercise for fattening the soul in a way that protects the vulnerable self, enhances feelings of well-being, and then—without even trying—contagiously overflows into the world. It all starts inside, with an inner plumpness. Try this exercise when you're feeling unhappy or angry or sad—or even better, as a daily spiritual practice to keep your soul plumped up and ready for those slings and arrows of everyday life, which, when they hit a plumped-up soul, might just bounce off—or at least not sting quite so much.

A Layer of Lovingkindness

Acknowledge that there is, within your soul or psyche, a suffering and vulnerable "child"—insecure, frightened, sad, lost, or confused. Or maybe your suffering child is presently throwing a tantrum, as you are feeling angry, jealous, greedy, lustful, envious, or even filled with murderous rage—and that's just your relatively tame *conscious* self. Not a pretty picture, but there it is. We are all sinners, as the Bible says. We are all suffering, as Buddhism says. Whatever religious or spiritual tradition we inhabit, we are reminded that human experience is painfully flawed. Some of us could use more contemplation along these lines. But others of us who tend to obsess over our flaws need to work towards acceptance of our imperfect selves and find liberation through forgiveness and affirmation. As Jay McDaniel says, "Some people need to say 'I have sinned' and others need to say 'I am beautiful.' Most of us need to say 'I have sinned and I am beautiful.'"[23]

So, for the first part of this mental exercise, think of that vulnerable part of your soul and imagine a soft, fat layer of lovingkindness gently surrounding the pain. I particularly like Thich Nhat Hanh's "suffering child" meditation and practice it when my own primitive inner child begins acting out or screaming bloody murder. He suggests that we try to evoke an image of ourselves at the age of five or six, and how we looked then. You might think of your first school picture and see yourself as you were then, right down to the shiny freckles and missing front teeth.

Breathing in, I see myself as a suffering child.
Breathing out, I care for myself as a suffering child.

You can add words of affirmation, too, such as "Even though I am imperfect (or sad or angry), I deeply and unconditionally love myself." For some, a line of poetry or scripture can help. After a few calming breaths of this suffering child meditation, you will begin to feel yourself relax into that warm, expansive layer of loving-kindness that protects and nurtures your best self. Like me, you might find it helpful to think about God in process-relational terms, the Soul of the world encircling your suffering child with divine empathy. I like this personal view of God as found in both my faith and in Whitehead's philosophy, yet it may not be for everyone. But for me, the sense of what Whitehead calls the "poet of the world" encircling me with lovingkindness enhances my experience of beauty and causes my soul to inflate with joy.

The Girth of Gratitude

Once you acknowledge your vulnerable self and are fattened up with that warm, encircling layer of loving-kindness, then you move to the really fun part of this exercise. Here you fatten up exponentially, because this part of the exercise allows you to indulge in gratitude as if it were chocolate cake or scones with clotted cream. It's okay to indulge, for gratitude expands the soul as nothing else can. Begin visualizing and naming the things you feel grateful for—the sky, the sea, the birds, the people you love, the joy of work well-done, a poem, a work of art, a joke, a laugh, a beloved pet, a kind word, a cup of tea.

With each naming, you can feel your spirit inflating until it reaches gigantean proportions.

Indulge Me

Now, being a philosopher above all things, I cannot let this gratitude experience pass unexamined, so indulge me a little further. If you reflect upon the things that make your heart soar, or stimulate a feeling of well-being—the things that make you, well, *happy*—you will find something really interesting: You will discover that the things you are looking at, envisioning, or naming in your gratitude exercise are not things at all, but rather experiences of beauty. It's not the cup of tea in itself for which I am grateful; it is the moment when the fragrance of the steaming tea wafting from a paper-thin china cup co-mingles with the stimulating book I'm reading, or the comfortable conversation I'm having with a friend. It's the moment, the becoming, the experience unfolding—the confluence of things that creates a sense of intense harmony in my soul. This brings us back full circle to the notion that a Fat Soul is, above all, a beautiful soul, a soul drenched in beautiful *becomings,* a soul that lives for beautiful moments, a soul that glides along the corridors of the universe with a God whose yearning for beauty—for intense, loving harmony—trumps all other desires of the divine heart.

Fat Soul, Happy Soul

This intentional expansion of the soul through lovingkindness and gratitude inevitably results in a pro-found sense of well-being.   Whitehead calls such intensely harmonious well-being "Beauty."   For he believed (in so many words), that when it comes to the soul, Big is Beautiful.

After practicing the soul-fattening exercise, you are now more in touch with not only the most painful part of yourself, but also with the most beautiful part of yourself, creating an intense harmonious moment in time. Your expanding soul feels more deeply connected to the expanding universe—to the very Soul of the universe—and so descends upon your soul that peace "which passes all understanding."

After this little exercise, you can now afford to be generous with others because you have so much. Even if you are a skinny person, you are big inside. You are HUGE. You are a walking balloon. If you don't give some of your gratitude and love away, you might burst!

In fact, you do burst. Yes, you explode! With every becoming moment, you are bursting something fresh into the world that wasn't there before. Your inner fatness adds another layer of beauty to the world. You will find yourself less sensitive to the criticisms of others, less angry, less depressed by circumstances. And it's all because you have allowed yourself a little self-indulgence into the healing realm of Big Happiness—a beautiful pursuit, indeed.

S-I-Z-I-N-G Up

Pursue Big Happiness. Don't settle for shallow substitutes. Discover the kind of happiness that thin, inhospitable souls cannot even imagine! Embrace it all, the beauty and the terror, the suffering and joy. Grow your soul with layer upon layer upon layer of compassion, beginning with yourself and then stretching outward to the whole wide world. Herein lies the secret of inner immensity.

Part Two
Fat Soul Planet

Spacious, Gracious Simplicity

'Tis the gift to be simple, 'tis the gift to be free
'Tis the gift to come down where we ought to be,
And when we find ourselves in the place just
right,
'Twill be in the valley of love and delight.
　　　　—from "Simple Gifts," a Shaker dance song

By God I mean a spacious receptacle—an Open
Space—within which the entire universe unfolds,
moment by moment.
　　　　　　　　　　　　　—Jay McDaniel

For a time I rest in the grace of the world, and am
free.
　　　　　　　　　　　　—Wendell Berry

　　A few years ago, my husband and I made a radical change in our lives. We sold our house, our cars, and everything we owned in the world—a half-century of accumulated stuff, offered to the highest bidder in a massive garage sale. We then packed some clothes and the remains of our worldly goods—favorite books, electronics, mementos, the bare essentials—into six slightly battered suitcases and headed south to the central coast of Ecuador.

　　Crazy? Yes, indeed. But here we are.

　　We simplified as people our age do, only in a more radical way so that we could try out an "encore career" in an exotic location. Thanks to technology, our chosen work as on-line teachers and writers could be done anywhere. And while we're at it, wouldn't it be nice to find a place where we could live out our values on a small budget? A place of beauty and simplicity—a place where, after a lifetime of work and hurry and clutter, we could focus on the soulfulness of a simpler life.

Moving to the Middle of the World

That's why, when we discussed various exotic-yet-affordable destinations, we took a serious look at this small Andean country straddling the equator, which happened to have just made a radical, pioneering leap of its own. Beginning in 2007, the new government of Ecuador created an unprecedented vision for the country, a return to indigenous wisdom: the Quechua way of *sumak kawsay,* translated, "life at its fullest."

S*umak kawsay*—life at its fullest—understands the world as interrelated. The Quechua people are friends with the mountains and birds and forests. Humans, for the Quechua, are viewed as only one part of a whole, a whole that is more than the sum of its parts. In this indigenous worldview, to harm nature is to harm humanity and violate the whole. Life at its fullest, then, consists of achieving total harmony with the community and with the cosmos.

Such a worldview values community, nature, and simplicity—a worldview with many spiritual cousins. One of them is process thought, based on the philosophy of Alfred North Whitehead, which sees the world as a web of relations. "Process thinking is concerned with the well-being of individuals and also with the common good of the world, understood as a community of communities of communities."[24] Whiteheadians would see the Quechua's "life at its fullest" as life at its most beautiful, that is, a life which seeks intense harmony not only for oneself, but also for the whole. So it is easy to see why two former ministers, educators, and process thinkers would be drawn to Ecuador's vision.

Radical Happiness

Even more radical, Ecuador took this philosophy—what they call a "cosmovision"—and made it policy. This translated into "happiness economics," a focus on uplifting the poor, improving quality of life, and creating a new constitution (2008) in which Ecuador became the first nation on earth to give rights to nature—yes, rivers and trees and wild monkeys and tree frogs have constitutional rights! Article 71 states: "Nature or *Pachamama*, where life is reproduced and exists, has the right to exist, persist, maintain and regenerate its vital cycles, structure, functions and its processes in evolution. Every person, people, community or nationality will be able to demand the recognitions of rights for nature before the public organisms."

But of course, in the real world such radical new vision does not materialize with ease. Since 2008, Ecuador has already experienced heartbreaking violations of nature's rights due to the machinations of politics, the addictive power of oil, and the hardscrabble world of economics. Nonetheless, the fact remains—a "stubborn fact," as Whitehead would say—that for the first time in history, a nation has dared to give constitutional rights to nature. And so, despite the inevitable ups and downs of such radical policy, it gives us hope that human consciousness does in fact evolve into greater awareness of our biological and spiritual connection to the earth and its creatures.

Falling into the Great Unknown

Our adventure into simplicity began with great deliberation and planning, but not without a sense that we would, at some point, have to let go and jump into the Great Unknown. Giving up everything familiar and starting over in a foreign country meant letting go to something very wide and mysterious—and risky—like jumping out of a plane and hoping your parachute opens. I won't pretend it was a smooth, gentle landing—anything but. As with all radical new beginnings, I felt utterly lost and rootless at first. Yet the sheer beauty of this country took me under its wing and, with time, I began to find my way.

So, that's how it happened: we just let go and fell—fell into simplicity, like one falls in love—and we are just that, in love with the simple life. I still wake up shocked by this fact, shocked that I feel so very rich.

Now that I live under the wide blue sky, free from a lifetime of clutter, I can finally breathe. And in the spaciousness of simplicity, not only can I breathe, but I can hear God breathing, too. I hear God breathing in the suspirations of the sea, the rising breath, the sigh of release, the loving embrace of all things living and dead and about-to-be born. I feel enfolded by a divine spaciousness and see things quite differently now.

Life in a Fishing Village

During our first couple of years, we lived in a tiny fishing village where everyone lives by the cycles of sun and moon and tide rather than by clocks and deadlines. Daily life moves and flows and trundles along with the gentle rhythms of the sea. Nothing is forced or fast. Electricity is not a thing to be taken for granted in such a village, and we often did without.

Choosing not to buy a car, we were driven around by a local mototaxi (a motorcycle with an open cab attached), allowing us freedom to stretch out and enjoy the calming effect of cows grazing on green hills, or, if we were lucky, the sudden rise of a snowy egret splaying its enormous white wings and flapping languidly up into the blue sky.

On my shopping excursions to pick up brightly colored fruits and vegetables from family-owned *tiendas*, my driver would address me as *Prima*, the Spanish word for a female cousin. And I, in return, called him *Primo*, for that's the common way of greeting people—as cousin. The villagers apparently feel that we are all in this together, and that we need to see ourselves as related, as an extended family of sorts. And for Ecuadorians, that includes the snowy egret, too.

A Chocolate Lover's Dream

We now reside in a seaside Ecuadorian city, still living quite simply on a small budget, arranging our lives around large doses of nature and equally large doses of locally grown foods. If I felt deprived, I would not (I confess) participate in this adventure, but I don't feel deprived in the least. Perhaps this is because one of the locally grown foods that supports small communities in Ecuador—including indigenous tribes in the Amazon—happens to be cacao. Ecuador is famous for its chocolate—and bananas. Not to mention papayas. With a life full of papayas and bananas and chocolate: who could ask for more?

In fact, I can now say with conviction that no matter where you live, the simple life is a good life, a happy life, one worthy of our imagination and energy and effort, even if it means a gradual letting go—one less car, one less closet full of clothes, one less commitment of time.

Simplifying your lifestyle may not be easy, but there is, with each letting go, a growing sense of spaciousness that transcends the smaller griefs. Simplicity carves out a fresh landscape within the soul, making room for things that matter. And, as it happens, these are not "things" at all, but enriching experiences and relationships and moments of intense beauty. Without so many *things* to distract, the landscape of the mind becomes clearer, calmer, more fluid and curious and open to novelty. It's all about learning to "rest in the grace of the world."

The Valley of Love and Delight

I'm not sure I would recommend anything quite so radical and psychically jolting as selling everything and moving to a fishing village in a foreign country. That is, one has to admit, a bit crazy. But idealists are a bit crazy, and if we are touched with idealism, there's nothing for it but to try to live out those ideals. I now feel a warm kinship with Henry Thoreau and Wendell Berry, and with all those who seek freedom in places where most people don't think to look.

And like other crazy people, I *know* things. At least I know things I did not—could not—know before, except in an abstract intellectual way. I have inner knowledge now, precious knowledge, for I have seen the Valley of Love and Delight, and it is real, and it is good. And it all has to do with the sky and the trees and the feeling you get when you pay attention to them.

I know now that the way to simplicity is to simply love the earth, to follow the snowy egret's rise into the blue sky, to laugh at the monkey, and to stand in awe at the sea's eternal undulations. Simplifying is not so much about doing without, but about finding riches in other places, deep places, wide-open places—places where we can hear God breathing.

S-I-Z-I-N-G Up

Less is more in a Fat Soul world. Life in Ecuador has taught me that simplicity nurtures the size of the soul, flexing the muscles of the spirit to replace the false comfort of things with the real comfort of a meaningful relationship to the earth, to each other, and to oneself. Simplicity is at the heart of Fat Soul—for without all the clutter, you can see higher, wider, and deeper. Simplicity makes us larger.

The Numinosity of Rocks

I do not know how I may seem to others, but to myself I am only a small child wandering upon the vast shores of knowledge, every now and then finding a small bright pebble to be contented with.
—Plato

I go treasure hunting on the beach at low tide, even when I should be doing other things. The tide calls and I respond, leaving unwashed dishes or half-written paragraphs. We live according to the tide here in El Matal, a quiet fishing village on the coast of Ecuador. At this particular spot on the equator—directly east of the Galapagos Islands—the warm tropical current from north meets a colder current from the south to create a rich bonanza for fishermen and shell seekers alike. But as serendipity would have it, we shell seekers often find even more beguiling treasures.

Small, mineral-rich rocks in variegated colors and designs wash up on the beach alongside giant conch shells and smooth driftwood. I stuff my pockets with what I can carry, pebbles and small rocks—red, orange, green, even pure crystal—until I am so weighed down I can hardly walk home. But I revel in each find like a child on an Easter egg hunt, plucking up the colorful little gems before the sea reclaims them. It's as if a Primordial Artist is sculpting away deep under the sea, tossing up imaginative, wholly original creations for the lucky treasure-seekers on shore.

The Spirit of Rocks

Why are we so drawn to rocks? Perhaps we are wired that way. Carl Jung viewed rocks as one of the primordial symbols of eternity. He said that each of us has inherited this ancient human tendency toward seeing–or rather, *feeling*–the sacredness in rocks. Primitive human beings believed that rocks were filled with gods and spirits. This is where we get the idea of piling rocks on graves or creating tombstones, which were once believed to contain the spirit of the loved one. In the same way, the earliest sculptors sought to "free the spirit" within the stone.

Whitehead, Buddhism, and quantum physics all agree (using their own language) that rocks are, in their essence, aggregates of vibrant energy rather than inert lumps of matter. As science pushes us forward, far beyond Newtonian physics and Cartesian dualism, it also circles back to something ancient and mysterious and primal. We can now appreciate with fresh eyes the "superstitions" of the ancients who felt a sense of "mystical participation" with nature. In this vein, process theologian David Griffin sees postmodernity as a time for the "re-enchantment" of nature.[25]

We can begin the re-enchantment process with something as simple as a rock. The energy of rocks is particularly mysterious and primordial. I love to pick up a small rock from the wet sand and feel its warmth in my hand, even on chilly, sweatshirt days when the clouds hang low and the volcanic sand cools my feet. A rock holds the energy of the sun long after everything around it succumbs to darkness and chill. The warm energy of the rock feels as if it were a living thing. And, in a sense, it is. And its "life" radiates a personality of something strong and trustworthy—and forever present in the world, remaining long after we are gone. The rock is very sure of itself, of its past and its future. And it has reason to be. When we pick up a rock, we are not just holding a lump of minerals: we are holding a piece of eternity in our hands.

The Comfort of Rocks

This deep symbolism of rocks sustains us, especially during grief. My husband and I recently lost a good friend, a bright and shining soul still in his prime. After hearing this news, I walked along the shore, feeling the intrepid tide pulling the sand out from under my feet, feeling as if the world were nothing but shifting sand. But then I turned my attention to the scattered rocks left behind on shore and they seemed to have another message. In the midst of perpetual perishing, there are solid things too, such as eternity and God's eternal care. A single rock can comfort. I found that day a special rock that seemed somehow to speak, to connect, to symbolize something of the spirit of the friend who passed away. Even now, just looking at that rock reminds me not only of the sturdy, steadying character of our friend–a "rock" in our lives–but of his eternal spirit that lives on, both in this world, and in the great mystery beyond. Eternity holds him.

Divinity speaks to us through the humble rock, as it takes on "numinosity," a term popularized by Rudolf Otto as meaning "awe-inspiring" or "holy." The word "numinous" was later adopted by Jung to refer to the unusual, heightened modes of awareness brought about by symbols (such as stones). These symbols return us to our most ancient psychic roots. So then, the rock speaks of something more than itself, a symbol of something deep and ancient and eternal.

Rocks are healing in that they connect us to something beyond our struggles and mortality. To remind us of this, we might get into the habit of carrying a favorite pebble in our pocket so that, during the vicissitudes of the day, we can reach for it, feel its solid, cool smoothness between our fingers and remember the Deep Eternal.

Watering Rocks

We can also find ways to create art with rocks or arrange rocks in our gardens, especially so that we can water them along with our plants. Water seems to "re-spirit" the rock. After one of my rock hunts, when I unload my pockets on the porch to examine my treasures, I realize that the very rocks that looked so dazzling and lively when wet with sea water, now look dull when dry. That's why beach rocks are so much more beautiful *in situ*. When we remove them, which of course we do—who can pass up a gleaming blue pebble?—the rocks lose something of their "spirit." So I put the smaller stones in a glass vase filled with water. The rocks smile back at me with their true colors and dramatic deep veins, and I feel their numinosity once again. The "living" rocks connect me to some deep eternal mystery, to the very divinity within all things.

The Solid Side of God

When I ponder the numinosity of rocks, I cannot help but think of God's eternal constancy in the midst of the everflowing movement of life. Yes, Heraclitus, all is flux; yet within that flux, we touch solid ground with the presence of divine love and suffering and creativity inside everything and everyone and every flowing moment. This is the solid side of God: the unwavering eternal love—our "Rock of Ages."

And in order not only to know, but also to *feel* the Deep Eternal, we need to allow ourselves a little re-enchantment now and then. To become like children. To be awed by the Primordial Artist beneath the sea, who is always there, forever tossing up pieces of eternity for those who seek after deep things.

S-I-Z-I-N-G Up

The earth is alive, vibrating on frequencies that we don't often tune into, except for those times that we are caught off-guard by enchantment. The earth loves us and wants to be in relationship with us. A soul that expands enough to treasure the beauty of rocks is a soul that knows the divinity of the earth—and will preserve the earth, pebble by pebble.

You, Me, and the Ceibo Tree

Unless someone like you cares a whole awful lot, nothing is going to get better. It's not.
                                        —Dr. Seuss

Some trees are more than trees; they are enchantresses. The ceibo is one such beguiler. The ciebo (pronounced, "say-bo") tree makes its home where I live, on the tropical coast of Ecuador, and it is only a short walk up an easy hill for me to find at least three striking ceibo trees, each of them singular and majestic and altogether enchanting.

And I am not the only one who thinks so. The Mayan culture in Central America believed that a single Great Ceibo tree inhabits the very center of the earth, uniting the earthly world with the spirit world above. Souls are transported to the heavens via the long, thick vines hanging down from the spreading limbs.

I can imagine this, can't you?

And in case you should want to travel to these parts and visit a ceibo tree in person, a word of caution is due: When you come upon a ceibo tree, whether on foot or on a bicycle or in a car, you must stop. You must stop and stare. You must stop and stare and remember to breathe, for you will be touched by its magic. It's unavoidable. The ceibo is a tree that charms its way right into the corneas of your eyes, travels down into your bloodstream, and even into your bones and muscles, and doesn't stop until it reaches your soul.

You cannot ignore a ceibo. The ceibo refuses to be overlooked, snubbed, or discounted as a mere tree. As I say, they are more than trees. Ceibos are the kings and queens of the dry tropical forest, dominating acacias, palms, and other "ordinary" trees. The ceibo, with its lime green trunk and spindly, fairy tale limbs is not ordinary. Oh, no. It lives and breathes and boasts and jokes and shouts out to all passersby: *I am Green, I am Beautiful, I am Ceibo!*

Yes, it's true. They do, in fact, shout those things— if you have the ears to hear.

In fact, around a ceibo tree, no imagination is safe. A ceibo may suddenly reach out to grab you with its gnarly finger-like limbs. Their smooth green bodies—or, trunks, to be precise—look like skin, human skin, only green.

They move, too. Honestly, some ceibo trees appear to be walking; others seem to be lurching forward or even dancing. They have a bit of the Grimm's Fairy Tale about them, as if they might just reach out and pick you up and stuff you inside the dark holes of their enormous trunks, perhaps to have you for lunch later in the day.

And if you look at them just right, they seem to be eyeing you with as much interest as you have for them.

Ceibos are trees with personality. And if they were, in fact, human, they would be old storytellers, the kind with resonate voices and large eyes who, during the exciting parts, gesticulate dramatically.

What kinds of stories would the ceibo tree tell?

Some of them would be funny, like how the monkey stole the banana right out of the back pocket of someone staring up at a ceibo tree, too entranced to know the monkey was there.

And they would tell some sad stories, too. For ceibos can take on a lonely look, for you often come across a wide expanse of pasture land with only one ceibo tree languishing alone. The story of the lonely ceibo would be about why the forests were cut down around them. You see, many trees in the dry tropical forest in these parts were cut down in order to make room for cattle to graze or for crops to be gown. This makes it hard for the monkeys and the big cats and the birds to find a place to live. It makes it hard for humans, too, since all those trees make a difference to the temperature of the fragile earth, a round colorful ball struggling to stay healthy. But sadly, many poor farmers see no other option but to cut down forests in order to feed their families.

But there are good stories, too, hopeful stories that make you smile. Like the story of the wise woman, who looks at the ceibo tree so long and hard that she decides, then and there, to grow more trees in the places where the forests used to be. To give the ceibos company, of course. And to give monkeys plenty of tree limbs to swing on, and to give people good air to breathe. And, because the ceibo tree stimulates the imagination, the wise woman thinks: Perhaps farmers could plant fast-growing trees—ordinary trees, of course—for furniture and boats and houses, and when the trees are big and ready to harvest, more trees will be planted, so that these tree farms can save both the farmer's family and the air we breathe. Many such good ideas have been planted in the minds of wise people by merely gazing at a ceibo tree.

Yes, many people do look at the ceibo tree and are not only transfixed, but transformed. That is, they want to make the world a better place for birds and frogs and jaguars, and farmers, and of course, for ceibos.

But why, you may ask, are the ceibos spared the sad fate of the other trees when the forests are cut down? It is true that the ceibos are almost always left standing when all else is cut down for the cows or the crops. Think of the Mayans, the ones who claim there is a Great Ceibo tree at the center of the earth, holding the earth and sky together. Well, the people in Ecuador think about that, too. Even the tribes in the Amazon jungle think of the ceibo tree as filled with gods and spirits! You don't cut down a tree like that.

The ceibo also tells us stories about how much we are alike—that is, humans and trees. It shows off its green "skin" and lively personality to remind us that we are all friends. We are all part of the same air, the same land.   We all spring from the same earth; we are all shimmering in our aliveness, bursting to tell each other our stories. We are friends, you see: you, me, and the ceibo tree.

S-I-Z-I-N-G Up

The Fat Soul sees things that others do not see. Children understand this, of course, but adults bent on the seriousness and miseries of life often miss the whole secret world of trees. It takes a widening of the soul to make room for such secret worlds. But in this time of planetary crisis, we need to wake up and widen out. The world would be more hospitable to trees if only we could make   room   in   our   souls   for   imagination   and enchantment and the belief that trees have stories to tell.

The S-I-Z-E of a Panama Hat

Art is not a thing; it is a way.

—Elbert Hubbard

Sometimes a hat is just a hat. But sometimes it's more. Sometimes a hat is a way of life, a community, an art form, a sustainable way to live and be productive and happy and secure in the world. In the case of the Panama hat—so famously *not* made in Panama, as I will shortly explain—we have a kind of straw hat that can, if we ponder it a bit, provoke a fresh image for spiritual well-being, both personal and planetary.

I can't help but think big, wide thoughts about straw hats because I am a Fat Soul philosopher who currently lives only a stone's throw from the epicenter of the famous Panama hat. And, no, it's not even close to Panama. Ecuador is the true home of the Panama hat. The humble village called Montecristi spills down a gentle mountain-side on the languid coast of Ecuador, and has for centuries carried on the tradition of making the finest hats in the world. They have graced the heads of presidents and kings and queens and movie stars and mobsters alike. To think that these hats are handmade by artisans who may work three months on one finely woven hat and sometimes up to six months—or even a year—on a single *superfino* hat, one of the finest and most sought-after hats in the world! And the work is painstaking, not pretty, and definitely not comfortable.

Mosquitoes and Spiders and Mud—Oh, My!

The making of a Panama hat starts in the mosquito-ridden, muddy equatorial rainforest not far from Montecristi. This small micro-climate square of jungle hosts not only insects that can kill you, but the special Panama hat palms called *toquilla*. The process of getting to this special straw is no picnic. The "master weaver," the most experienced and revered artist in the village, does not send someone else to fight the mosquitoes and mud and spiders. He (so far, all male) goes himself—he has to, because only a master weaver can spot the right shoot, the *cogollo,* which has to be just the right age and plumpness. It's a labor of love—not for the faint of heart—to find the raw materials for a Panama hat.

A Very Touchy Subject

Now, about the name. It's a very touchy subject down here. Really. My Ecuadorian friends bristle at the name "Panama" hats, insisting on calling them Montecristi hats or *sombreros pajas de toquilla* (straw hats of *toquilla*). However unfair and egregious this misnomer, the name "Panama" hat sticks. How do we account for such a travesty?

History is a funny thing. As it turns out, the California Gold Rush is to thank for this *faux pas.* Back in the mid-1800s, if you suffered from gold rush fever in New York or anywhere on the east coast, the most efficient way to get to California was to take a ship down to Panama, take a donkey ride (or whatever) across the narrow isthmus, and hop aboard another ship to take you to up to California. During your donkey ride (or whatever) across the isthmus of Panama, you would encounter dozens of smiling vendors, all peddling straw hats sent up from Ecuador. Seeing as you're half-dead with heat exhaustion due to a blazing sun, you snap up that straw hat—and besides, you will need it when you get to sunny California.

So, while the California '49ers were standing knee deep in the American River swapping Wild West stories over their sieves, Ecuadorian vendors were sending more hats up to Panama to be peddled to more adventurers crossing the isthmus on the way to get rich in California. Brilliant!   Except that when your fellow gold-panner asked, "Where'd you get that hat?" you'd say, "Panama." And later, with the construction of the Panama Canal—most especially that dapper photo of Teddy Roosevelt donning a straw hat—well, there you go. Thank you, Mr. President. "Panama hat" it is and will always be until the end of time.

Planetary Lessons from a Panama Hat
Once giving shade and style to gold-panning and get-rich-quick schemes and canals for Captains of Industry, today the Panama hat offers a broad-brimmed smile when it tells *the other side* of its story, the story of its home, its real home in the artisan community of Montecristi: a humble village that eluded the industrial revolution and modernity and pollution and the raping of our natural resources. Yes, the straw hat may have aided others on their way to "a better way of life," but its hometown totally missed the boat. While everyone up in California was having a party as they filled their pockets with gold, the village of Montecristi remained the same, weaving one hat at a time—and sending them up to Panama. How could a hat be so backwards? What was it thinking?

It wasn't thinking much, except how happy it was. It was at home on the balmy coast of Ecuador surrounded by good families who made the artistry of hat their pride and joy. For as long as recorded history, someone in the village of Montecristi, Ecuador, was busy weaving a hat. The biggest thing that happened in the life of the Panama hat was in the sixteenth century when the Spanish Conquistadors came to town bossing everyone around, influencing the shape of the hat—formerly more of a headdress or helmet-looking contraption—into a more European-style hat.

And now it seems that the rest of the world—having barely survived the ravages of modern industrialism, unfettered capitalism, Ayn Rand novels, and globalization—has come around full circle. The humble, organic, sustainable way of life built around a village of hat weaving artisans, seems super-cool—because it *is* super-cool. Suddenly, the old ways become a wave of the future, a "better way of life"—ironic, in the best sense. The Montecristi artisans represent an organic, sustainable art form which highlights a culture, a heritage, a way of life—something that can inspire people around the world as they seek sustainable communities of their own, communities that have personality and art and flair and a sense of purpose in the world.

The Style of Soul

In terms of spirituality, the Montecristi way of life can inspire us toward thinking in terms of quality of life rather than quantity of things, a way of life that promotes simplicity and beauty and pluri-cultural centers within a larger whole. In the case of Montecristi, we see the beauty of diversity, the richness of experience, the value of craft, of art, and tramping through muddy rainforests to find just the right shoots for creating something both beautiful and useful.

That one, slender green shoot quivers in the mottled light of the rainforest, catching the eye of the master weaver, the one who can envision this unremarkable shoot as the raw material for a thing of beauty. I believe that God is like this, like the master weaver who, with divine imagination, goes deep into the world to find just the right possibility to offer the next moment of creation. This divine presence, the Soul of the world, does not reside in a cushy supernatural existence, bossing people around from on high, but nestles in the shoots and stalks and butterflies and spiders and people and monkeys, and even in the sweltering, muddy, jungle-like parts of life.

This cosmic Master Weaver is wise to the ripe, plump, tender possibilities for transformation within all things, even as we plow right over them in blundering stupidity. But we can stop and look and learn from the Master Weaver how to spot these fresh shoots of possibility and co-create something beautiful in the world. Perhaps communities built on arts and crafts can show us the way. In these discouraging days of global warming, we are in need of something protective, something beautiful, something woven out of the earth itself.

S-I-Z-I-N-G Up

A Fat Soul kind of world stretches itself toward novelty and diversity, because every place on earth has something hugely important to offer the whole. Fat Souls know the power of arts and crafts to make the world more soulful, more sustainable, more beautiful—not to mention, more stylish.

Changing the World
One Bite at a Time

One of the greatest opportunities to live our values—or betray them—lies in the food we put on our plates.
—Jonathan Safran Foer

I am convinced that animal compassion is one of the next great spiritual awakenings.
—Ronald L. Farmer

Sometimes, it all seems too much. Taking stock of my world, with its unabated horrors cavalcading across my television screen, its never-ceasing injustices, its apathy in the face of our ecological crisis, its penchant for sensational side shows that distract us from these realities—well, it's enough to make me throw myself, hand on brow, onto my fainting couch. Which is, I regret to say, a metaphorical fainting couch, since I don't have the privilege of owning one.

Is it just me?

If you, too, experience occasional bouts of soul-wilting despair over the planet and its sorrowful inhabitants, let me offer you some smelling salts: get up and do something about it.

But what? you say. What I can do? I am a tiny blip of dust on the cosmic scene. I can do nothing of significance.

Oh, but you can.

I Can't Believe They Used to Eat Animals

One simple—but hugely significant—thing you can do to alleviate suffering and save the planet to boot is to become a vegetarian. This is a life-altering decision, and I don't blame you if you hesitate. It took me ages to get there myself. Back in my university days, I even wrote a paper in a philosophy seminar arguing *against* vegetarianism, with cogent arguments to back me up! There are many ways the mind rationalizes what it wants to be true, all of which, in the light of lovingkindness, turn out to be tinkling cymbals.

I realize from my own experience that the older you are, the more difficult the transition to vegetarianism; in some situations, it may not be feasible. But my hope is that the Millennials, who are acutely sensitive to animal suffering and environmental issues, will take the ball and run with it (and hopefully figure out a meat alternative for my cat). Yes, future generations will indeed shake their heads and say: I can't believe they used to eat animals!

Saving Souls

On a spiritual note, a vegetarian diet can awaken us to fresh landscapes of compassion and understanding that enlarge the soul. Professor Ron Farmer, a biblical scholar (and my vegetarian husband), wrote in a recently published essay, "I am convinced that animal compassion is one of the next great spiritual awakenings."[26] He brings up the curious mistranslation in the Genesis creation stories of the Hebrew *chay nephesh*. This expression literally translates as "living souls." However, when the phrase refers to animals rather than humans, it is invariably mistranslated "living creatures," which belies our ongoing, historical bias against animals as living *souls*.

Animals are living souls, just like us. Yes, they vary in levels of awareness and complexity, which we need to take into account. For example, if I were forced to choose, I would eat a chicken before I would eat a pig—

for we now know that pigs are highly intelligent creatures, on par with dolphins and smarter than dogs, yet they do not share the same legal protections because we want our bacon.

In light of this, how can vegetarianism become a spiritual adventure? While I invite you to do your own research, here are three soul-expanding facts to consider:

- I can save AT LEAST one life per day! It is estimated that a single vegetarian saves between 371 and 582 animals per year.[27] Wow. That's what I call "saving souls"—for remember, farm animals and humans alike are *chay nephesh,* living souls.
- I will be saying NO to cruelty. Ten billion farm animals now live in tortuous conditions inside factory farms. (To say more about the grim realities of slaughter houses and factory farms sends me back to the fainting couch.) By abstaining from meat, I will be joining a host of other compassionate souls out there who choose to practice nonviolence in their everyday lives.
- I will be saying YES to the planet. While statistics differ, it is an unavoidable fact that livestock production is *one of the worst single factors* in the degradation of the environment. So, by simply choosing what I put on my plate, I can help create a sustainable future for generations to come. In this way, I am stretching my soul forward into a future filled with stars.

Of course, if you're not ready to follow me—not to mention Paul McCartney and millions of other very cool people—into a vegetarian lifestyle, you can start by simply eating *less* meat and going free-range when you do. Many of my non-vegetarian friends are choosing this alternative—a massive step forward.

And that's what it's all about, moving forward *in whatever way you can* to alleviate suffering and promote environmental well-being.

I became a vegetarian not for the sake of my health, but for the sake of my soul—and for the Soul of the world. For in my philosophy, all creatures great and small have a soul; they are each inhabited by the Soul of the world—that divine presence in all things. And so, to make room for all these souls, we need to make the circle wider. We don't need to fatten our cows with growth hormones; we need to fatten our souls with compassion.

The Onus Is on Us

Alfred North Whitehead, the father of process philosophy, said way back in 1929: "But whether or no it be for the general good, life is robbery. It is at this point that with life morals become acute. The robber requires justification."[28] That means the onus is on us. We have to *justify* our taking of life. Knowing what we know now, can we justify the killing of animals for the sake of our dining enjoyment?

For the awful truth is that farm animals today are viewed as "units of production" rather than living souls who suffer. And yet, we are all made of the same stuff: you, me, the ceibo tree—and cats and dogs and pigs and cows, too. To separate some of these animals into "things" with no intrinsic value, no real feeling, is part and parcel of the mechanistic worldview that we are slowing and painfully growing out of as science, philosophy, and morals evolve. Let's just hope our life on this planet does not end before we get there.

S-I-Z-I-N-G Up

There are many ways to save the planet and lessen the amount of suffering in the world. Choosing to be a vegetarian is one of them. Albert Schweitzer, one of the greatest Fat Souls in history said, "Until he extends the circle of his compassion to all living things, man will not himself find peace." So just say NO to factory farms and

YES to expanding your soul to include the well-being of the "least of these" in the animal world.

Don't Just Hug a Tree: Be a Tree

Everybody who's anybody longs to be a tree.

—**Rita Dove**

These days I think of myself in terms of *treeness*. Trees have somehow waylaid me—gotten into my blood, wormed their way into my dreams, planted themselves in circles around my mind. These curvaceous sirens of scent and sap and flagrant wildness can get to you in whatever shape or form. Who can resist a spreading acacia, a flowering dogwood, a purple jacaranda? Who does not swoon at the sight of a weeping willow? Or is not captured by the fairy-tale magic of the ceibo tree? Not to mention the come-hither sway of a languid palm.

You know you can't resist.

They stop you dead in your tracks. In fact, I often try to imagine *being* a tree, and how wonderful it must feel to be still and stately and beautiful and so very rooted in the earth.

It's good to think of yourself in terms of treeness, and I'll tell you why: Trees are the guardians of the earth, standing watch over creation in clusters or alone, in winter or summer—barren or blooming. They just stand. But it's an active kind of standing. Change defines the tree's very existence: a cherry blossom here, a ripening plum there, a new bud, a green sprout—even the gnarly trunk grows gnarlier with age. And one cool morning, a verdant leaf, quite used to basking in its silky green softness, wakes up to find itself brittle and golden—and barely hanging on.

And all of these goings-on happen in the surest of all knowledge that change will continue, unrelenting. Even in the tropics where I live now, the trees never quit moving within their stillness, growing barren and stoical in the dry season only to become giddy and emerald and fruit-bearing during the rainy season. All this change means that life is not easy for the tree. There will be droughts or floods or worse, lightening, the ax, or—heaven help us—the conflagration. Bad things do happen to trees—ask the Lorax from Dr. Seuss, he'll tell you. But despite all these facts of life and death, the trees of the world still stand as monuments to stillness-within-change, a moving magnificence, and who would not like to be just that?

But don't think it's all for show. The tree doesn't just stand around looking pretty. Creatures on two legs and four depend on it for breathing—for the very oxygen of life; high up in its leafy branches, a robin delivers fresh worms to open-mouthed young; a blackbird sings opera from a bouncing twig; a sulky child climbs its trunk seeking refuge from the world of adults; in summer heat, an old cow luxuriates in the tender mercies of its shade; young lovers roll together under its discreet canopy; monks and seekers and Buddha himself find enlightenment under its boughs.

And all the while the infinitesimal changes of the tree burst forth—a democracy of countless explosions of energy, alive and swirling together into a singular burgeoning beauty.

The tree is a noun within a verb, a gerund of perfect equanimity—and that is one reason to be a tree, a very good reason when you think about it. Who doesn't crave a little equanimity? You can take any tree you want, any season, and simply be that tree. The whole key to being a tree is what you do *not* see, that is, what lies beneath in the loamy darkness below. Its roots burrow down deep for nourishment and stability, for here in this dark and restful place peace reigns, even in the painful season—even when winter's cruelty strips all its leafy loveliness away. During those stark times, when life on the surface has left the tree vulnerable and fruitless, the invisible roots speak to it of spring in the nurturing voice of Julian of Norwich: *all shall be well, and all shall be well, and all manner of things shall be well.*

Many people these days only believe in what they see, as if only the surface of things really matters. They live in forgetfulness of roots. They forget Helen Keller who found peace in the depths of total darkness, in the rootedness of herself and in the embrace of an invisible, dark, loving God. For the dark richness of a rooted life brings out one's soul, one's spiritual moorings.

When I was a young minister in a Gothic-style church with congregants awaiting some message from my unsteady voice, I was saved into confident equanimity by the Tree of Life tapestry hanging over the sanctuary door, reminding me of my purpose and my roots. Without that tree to root me to the floor, to the pulpit, to my message, I might have fainted straightaway. Even now, I write with a tapestry of a tree above my writing table, for without it I might never have the courage to write a single word.

Every great religion and philosophy and mythology holds the tree dear—a sacred symbol for the interconnection of all life. But do we think enough about the roots? How they go deep and wide and connect to other roots even when, on the surface of things, the trees seem impossibly separate and starkly alone. Perhaps, from time to time, we need to simply rest quietly in the nourishing darkness of our roots.

One breath is all you need to be a tree: (Breathing in) "I am a beautiful tree." (Breathing out) "I am rooted in peace." That's it—one breath; it's easy.

You will see it all in that breath—your treeness, your magnificence, and your rootedness in the mysterious web of life. And if you do this often enough, if you breathe yourself into a tree, something wonderful happens. Your colorful, changeable, surfacy life of wind and rain and sunshine and sorrow gives way to your quiet, deeper self within the nourishing womb of the earth. Here, peace awaits—whether we name it God or Christ or Buddha or Tao or Heaven or Allah or Mother Earth or simply Peace.   Peace, says Alfred North Whitehead, is "that Harmony of Harmonies, which calms destructive turbulence . . ." and "enlarges the field of attention."[29] In the dark embrace of Peace, everything goes wide, and we know that we are no longer alone.

This is what it means to be a tree: to know ourselves as beautiful in our particularity, but also to know that we are part of something deeper and wider— and loving. Especially loving. To know our treeness is to know that we are a part of the bark and the sap and the sprouting and the soil; it is to know that we are made up of the same ultimate stuff as trees—quivering flashes of purpose and beauty and unrelenting bursting-forths of fresh possibilities, one right after another.

S-I-Z-I-N-G Up

If we can practice being a tree, it is inevitable that we will fall hopelessly in love with trees, and not only with trees, but with the birds and cows and monkeys and everything that finds refuge in or under a tree. Maybe this is the beginning of something—something more than mysticism and symbolism, more than even our own equanimity. Maybe this is the key to saving the trees and the air and the rivers—and even ourselves. For trees are beautiful and hospitable and endlessly beguiling; trees are Fat Souls with roots and charm. Who, indeed, would not want to be tree?

Part Three
Fat Soul Luminaries

A Beautiful Madness

And now I understand
What you tried to say to me
How you suffered for your sanity
How you tried to set them free . . .
. . . I could have told you Vincent
This world was never meant
For one as beautiful as you
                    —Don McLean, "Starry Starry Night"

Perhaps the world was not meant for someone as beautiful as Vincent van Gogh—or perhaps it was. Perhaps, at the heart of things, Vincent was exactly what the world was meant to be.

Vincent came from a harsh Calvinist background. His father was a harsh Calvinist minister and Vincent was expected to follow suit in a harsh Calvinist world. He tried and he failed. Vincent's early adult life was a slow and painful coming-to-terms with the knowledge that he could never survive the narrowness thrust upon him. His church vocation limited his attention to the Bible and to the authority of tradition. Literature, art, and nature were viewed as dangerous distractions. But these were the very things Vincent craved. He craved largeness and breadth and beauty. He craved something wider if he were to survive; that is, he needed to expand his soul in order to save it.

And then it came, the break, the cracking of the chrysalis, the flight toward wideness and beauty. And as it turned out, love saved him, not a specific love but the love of "many things," as he wrote in a letter to his brother Theo: "I think that the best way to know God is to love many things"[30] And that is when he pledged himself to be an artist. As Cliff Edwards says in his remarkable work *Van Gogh and God: A Creative Spiritual Quest,* "Vincent suddenly and unexpectedly broke away from the narrow path of religious exclusivity and described a new path that saw not threatening distraction but strength in 'loving many things' . . . Vincent's search for the unification of nature, art, literature, religion, and practical service among the poor realized itself in a new phase of his religious transformation."[31]

Vincent was a deeply spiritual man. As he wrote to Theo, "You need a certain dose of inspiration, a ray from on high, that is not in ourselves, in order to do beautiful things."[32] Vincent loved God, he loved God deeply, and came to think of God as "not dead or stuffed but alive, urging us to love again with irresistible force—that is my opinion."[33] He saw God as a struggling Artist like himself—something Cliff Edwards says has "interesting parallels" with Whiteheadian process philosophy. I think Edwards is on to something as I expressed in the essay, "Van Gogh's God."[34] I also see how Vincent's spirituality of love, wideness, and intensity of feeling mirrors Whitehead's philosophy of beauty. Vincent's own soul—a kind of beautiful madness—found soothing peace on canvas and teaches us something of the meaning of beauty, and of the wideness beauty needs in order to breathe.

Many of us can identify with Vincent's stretch towards largeness of purpose, toward bigness of soul, even toward what I call the Fat Soul, the soul which dares to widen enough to "love many things" even at the risk of the uncomfortable and discordant—like loving your enemy (Jesus was a Fat Soul), like compassion and mindfulness (Buddha was a Fat Soul), like standing up to the meanest of fundamentalists (Malala Yousafzai is Fat Soul), or daring to challenge the boundaries of long tradition for the sake of love (Pope Francis is a Fat Soul).

A Fat Soul is a beautiful soul, a daring soul, a loving soul, a Vincent van Gogh kind of soul—a soul that "loves many things."

But such an expansive, Vincent-style soul—the beautiful soul—comes at a price: It must somehow integrate, harmonize, and transform the discordant and contrasting elements that accompany a soul that "loves many things."   Vincent's discordant elements plagued him his entire life, and this is important to beauty. "The Discord of the Universe," says Whitehead in *Adventures of Ideas*, "arises from the fact that modes of Beauty are various, and not of necessity compatible. . . . Wide purpose is in its own nature beautiful by reason of its contribution to the massiveness of experience."[35]   In other words, "to know God is to love many things."

So it seems to Vincent and to Whitehead and to Fat Soul philosophy in general, that the soul—and civilization itself—must continually move toward "massiveness," toward loving many things in order not only to keep from going cold and sterile, but also to allow discordant elements enough space for creating beauty out of the differences, the incompatibilities—even the wreckage.   And wreckage abounds.   But we are often afraid of "many things" especially when narrowness feels safe and secure.   We are afraid of things we don't understand, of new ideas, of other religions, of love and death and our own contradictory desires—we are fearful creatures on the whole.   Some elements of discord are evil, too.   "Discord may take the form of freshness or hope, or it may be horror or pain," says Whitehead.[36]

How on earth can anything beautiful come out of all that?

Vincent shows us how.   He shows us with "Flaming flowers that brightly blaze / Swirling clouds in violet haze," and with "Weathered faces lined in pain."[37] He shows us how to blend and shade and use both the light and the darkness to transform the discord into fresh forms of beauty.   He shows us how to paint outside the tradition, how to expand our souls, how to become co-creators with the loving and struggling Artist of the world. In short, he shows us by his life and his work what it means to transform raw pain into tragic beauty.

Vincent suffered from bouts of depression most of his life. Some theorize he later battled what we now call bi-polar disorder, or perhaps his troubles were due to a brain lesion aggravated by his use of absinthe—theories of his illness (and even his death) abound. But what we do know is that despite his illness, he was able to create extraordinary works of art in the ten years before his death. And in a profoundly spiritual way, his genius had something to do with his inner blooming—his movement from narrowness to wideness for the sake of love and beauty. I believe that this triumphant part of Vincent's story needs to be remembered against the more colorful mythology of "the tortured artist." It may be the very thing he tried to say to us.

We cannot forget that his art, his post-impressionist brilliance, would never have come into existence without an inner burgeoning towards "loving many things." Without Vincent's painful but necessary spiritual metamorphosis, there would be no "Starry Night" at all, only a sad and troubled man.

Vincent's short life—so eccentric and strange and troubled—may have ended in tragedy, but it was, I believe, a singularly beautiful life. Vincent's life tells us something of the nature of beauty; it tells the story of the universe itself. Whitehead says, "At the very heart of the nature of things, there are always the dream of youth and the harvest of tragedy. The Adventure of the Universe starts with a dream and reaps tragic beauty."[38]

Our lives are filled with tragedy because we are human, because we have the capacity to feel and love and risk and make choices—and suffer mental illness, too. Our lives may not always be happy or successful or "on track," but they can be beautiful nonetheless. And that just might be the point of it all.

S-I-Z-I-N-G Up

Fat Souls are sometimes filled with so much feeling that they naturally overflow onto a canvass or a page or a garden. In this way, suffering of mind or body can find creative transformation. Artists are naturally spacious souls who dare to dream of utterly fresh—and sometimes startling—ways of painting feeling. The world needs this kind of novelty, this kind of beauty, this kind of feeling. It all starts by "loving many things."

The Pope's Favorite Verb

Let yourself be 'merc'd.
                                                        —Pope Francis

Words have personality; they come and go out of fashion. Take the word "mercy." A bit old-fashioned, a little shop-worn, a tad dusty. Now, what if "mercy," a word many spiritual folk have politely shelved, could be resurrected? Is there any hope for "mercy"? Alas, if only it didn't just sit there looking archaic. If only it weren't a boring noun, but lively and vigorous as a verb. But wait, it is a verb! Pope Francis (Jorge Mario Bergoglio) has made it so. According to Austen Ivereigh[39], author of the Pope's biography *The Great Reformer*, "Bergoglio liked the way Latin had 'mercy' as a verb, *miserando*, and so created the Spanish *misericordiando*—an activity of the divine, something God does to you. '*Dejáte misericordiar*,' he would tell the guilt-ridden and the scrupulous, 'let yourself be mercy'd.'"

"Let yourself be 'mercy'd.'" Nice. It reminds me of an old grandma's hand-on-heart exclamation, "Mercy me!" Now, if only we had an example of this "verb" to burst forth from our merciless world of war, planetary destruction, and economic injustice. But wait, we do! Pope Francis himself is doing that very thing. He is vigorously showing us how to *mercy* the world.

While unapologetically upsetting the status quo with his relentless passion for the poor, the planet, and for the transformation of an economic system that creates havoc on both, Pope Francis puts mercy back into our vocabulary. But not as a noun. Rather, Pope Francis has single-handedly transformed an old-fashioned, dead-beat noun into a lively, active—albeit, somewhat subversive—verb.

In short, the Pope rocks.

Thanks to Pope Francis, mercy is a now a verb; he has given mercy legs to run. And we are all invited into this activity of mercy—all of us, Catholic, Protestant, Jew, Muslim, Hindu, nonreligious—we are all invited to be part of this divine activity of *mercying* the world.

The Pope sees mercy as the most salient feature of God's *activity* in the world. In other words, Pope Francis believes in verbs, in divine *activity*, not just ideas that sit around getting dusty.

As a process thinker, I can't help but feel a spiritual kinship, for the great process philosopher Alfred North Whitehead wrote not of a remote noun-like God, but rather of an active, loving, suffering, transforming God who is "the great companion—the fellow-sufferer who understands."[40] In the process worldview, everything is a verb—the whole world of becoming, from rocks to stars to people: everything is a verb. Including God.

It's a Copernican revolution of sorts, to think of the world—and God—in terms of verbs. Just as God, long ago, got lost in a noun of self-thinking thought (Aristotle), so *mercy,* through the centuries, became a fossilized noun: nice for display, but no longer alive. Well, now it is.

So "let yourself be mercy'd." It's not a trendy new malapropism, but rather old wisdom resurrected. It is the way of Jesus, the way of Buddha, the way of Torah, the way of Allah, the way of compassion. And now, as we witness a pope who continues to galvanize the world with his bold bent toward mercy for the poor and for the planet, we—all of us—are blessed to be mercy'd by his voice.

S-I-Z-I-N-G Up

Pope Francis is much beloved in the country of Ecuador. When he visited here in 2015, thousands turned out to see him. The woman who cuts my husband's hair beamed as she told us of taking her disabled aunt to see "Papa Francisco" in the city of Guayaquil. The aunt was given, among the thousands of worshippers, special attention—and a rose—by the Pope himself, as is his way. He is drawn to those who are the most vulnerable. The Pope is simply practicing what he believes is the way of Jesus. This is the way of all Fat Souls, from every religious background. They don't just talk about compassion—or mercy; they practice it. They pay attention to those most in need. Fat Souls, then, are not immovable nouns, but active verbs, always seeking new ways to incarnate love and beauty into the world.

Mozart's Beauty Secret

At the heart of the nature of things, there are always the dream of youth and the harvest of tragedy. The Adventure of the Universe starts with the dream and reaps tragic Beauty . . . . That the suffering attains its end in a Harmony of Harmonies.

—Alfred North Whitehead

**As an accompaniment to this essay, you may wish to listen to the last movement of Mozart's "Jupiter" Symphony.

What can we really say about beauty? If ever we could encapsulate beauty into a definition even remotely adequate, we might have to turn to music rather than words. For real beauty is not an abstract concept (forgive me, Plato); it is an experience—a complex, rich, large experience—one that defies being tied down by language. We might simply point to Mozart's Symphony No. 41 in C—the "Jupiter"—and be done with it. After listening to the last movement of the "Jupiter," having experienced the entrancing counterpoint melodies colliding into one another until you think your brain might explode with joy—well, what more can one say? As another great composer Robert Schumann said in 1835, "About many things in this world there is simply nothing to be said— for example, about Mozart's C-Major symphony with the fugue, much of Shakespeare, and some of Beethoven."[41]

But still we resort to words and analysis, grappling and groping for a string of phrases that might circle bashfully around the mystery of Mozart's genius. It's as though Mozart had an inside track to the heart of beauty—not all by himself, of course, but in relation to the host of composers before him, the exigencies of his personal situation, and the anticipation of what was to come. So it's not that beauty begins and ends with Mozart; he did not simply drop down from heaven. There is much of Bach in Mozart and Josquin des Prez and all the way back to Gregorian Chant. But Mozart had a singular voice—"the voice of God," as the character of the jealous Salieri painfully admits in *Amadeus*.[42]

But why? We want to understand *why* his music is beautiful—why it calms us, stirs us, challenges us—and how such beauty might seep into the cracks and crevices of our lives, how it can make us freer, our world more hospitable—even satisfy our personal spiritual yearnings in a belief in Something More. And maybe, too, how it can save us from ourselves. Beauty can do that; it can save us from our smallness and lack of vision and our impossible and impoverishing demands that life be limited to one key—and to hell with competing melodies.

Whiteheadian Beauty

Beauty of this kind—Mozart's kind, the complex and contrapuntal kind—shines out from the center of the philosophy of Alfred North Whitehead. He, too, had a special genius of his own and a revolutionary philosophy that regarded Beauty (with a capital B) as the very teleology of the universe. He viewed Beauty as harmony, yes, but not as easy-listening harmony; rather, he believed that Beauty is created out of rich and complex intensity of feeling, a feeling that can only emerge from the co-mingling of contrasting elements—a "Harmony of Harmonies." Whitehead believed in a contrapuntal view of life—many melodies woven together. Such Beauty brings about new life forms in the world, diverse planets and galaxies, and people like Mozart who can compose with "the voice of God."

Experiencing such Harmony of Harmonies is to know God—the God of Whitehead—the Soul of the world who feels everything. For this God "dwells in the tender elements in the world, which slowly and in quietness operate by love."[43] This divine love does not control everything that happens in the world, much of it evil. Rather, Whitehead's God, a relational God, feels everything, suffers everything, and transforms our sufferings into tragic Beauty. Whitehead's thought, like Mozart's symphony, is revolutionary. And like the last movement of Mozart's "Jupiter," so too the last part (Part Five) of Whitehead's *Process and Reality* can easily be described as "mind-blowing." There, Whitehead brings it all together: a visionary fugue of musical becoming—a revolutionary view of God and the world that is melodic and poetic, complex and unprecedented.

Suffering Beauty

The revolutionary visions of Whitehead and Mozart tell us that to know God is to know love—love within an expansive, rich, Harmony of Harmonies: somewhere in that experience lies the meaning of Beauty. Perhaps, even, the meaning of life.

But sorrow lives there, too. Despair and grief and longing find a home in Beauty. Whitehead developed his understanding of a suffering, relational God who lures the world toward Beauty following the death of his son in WWI. Mozart wrote the "Jupiter," his last symphony, while Austria was at war with Turkey. Personally he was suffering poverty, debt, and insuperable grief from the loss of his baby daughter. With sorrow as his companion, Mozart created Symphony No. 41—revolutionary beauty, godlike beauty—later dubbed the "Jupiter" (the Roman god). For in the last movement, something extraordinary happens. It had never happened before, and never since—not like this.

Godlike Beauty

In the last movement of the Jupiter, five separate melodies—not two or three, but five distinct melodies!—not only exist together but play together, tumbling toward each other and away again, daring one another, touching one another, challenging one another until, finally, they give up the chase and simply sound together all at once. At once! The many become one in the final fugal coda. As Mozart scholar Robert Levin explains in an interview on NPR, "At the very, very end, he does something absolutely unimaginable, which is that he combines all five of these tunes simultaneously, tossing them about from one instrument to the other in a display of intellectual fireworks that remains unprecedented in this symphonic domain."[44]

The Secret

But this unprecedented fugue is no chaotic free-for-all. Harmony exists. But how? The secret is this: there is something at the center of the co-mingling melodies, a four-note motif or theme that somehow makes the whole thing work. This simple thematic melody allows the four other melodies to express themselves contrapuntally with a sense of meaning and connection, each melody playing off the motif melody with its own spirited voice. Without this motif (which pervades the entire symphony), all would be chaotic dissonance.

Mozart as Metaphor

As a metaphor for Whitehead's concept of Beauty, we could say that in this final fugue, the four-note motif acts as the presence of God, holding the contrasting elements together and inviting each particular melody to be itself-in-relation. God is present in the moment—not outside looking in, not apathetic and remote. Rather, Whitehead would say that God is present in every moment of self-creation. And God unfolds with the music, luring all the other contrasting elements toward a rich harmony. The lure of God—the motif—is there, always, elegant and whole. And it loves many melodies.

We can play this metaphor many ways, such as the moments in our own lives, unfolding with sensitivity to the lure of God, finding psychic integration and intense harmony among all the competing feelings and possibilities within. We can see the larger picture, too: the melodies of the earth, of humanity, the cosmos. Some melodies are quiet introverts, others, jovial extroverts; some are snowy egrets, others are bees; there are melodies for the deeply religious and the skeptical, the athletic and the disabled, gay/straight, East/West, the planets and galaxies themselves. God lures them all toward the highest possible beauty, not only for themselves as particular melodies, but for themselves-in-relation to the whole symphony. In this way, the last movement of the "Jupiter" is a metaphor for life at its most beautiful—the many become one in a loving "concrescence" of creative contrasts.

Beauty Can Save Us

Is it any wonder that Woody Allen says that the "Jupiter" Symphony proves the existence of God?[45] After all, five melodies all playing together in the fugal coda is too much for any human to take in! Only God can grasp such profound complexity.

It's true. God's soul can feel everything in itself; we, on the other hand are limited. But we can develop wider, deeper, more beautiful souls—souls too big for repetitive, uninteresting melodies. We can even become what I call Fat Souls. To be a Fat Soul in a world sequestered in certainties and protected by walls of ignorance and fear and conformity is, no doubt, a counter-cultural melody. Perhaps that is exactly what the world needs.

S-I-Z-I-N-G Up

Mozart offers us a glimpse of God's vision for the world—a metaphor for how beauty can save us, our planet, our polarized rigidity in politics and religion, and the bifurcation of nature. And he does all this without words! Imagine. Mozart and Whitehead offer us, albeit in different "languages," a glimpse of the wideness of Beauty: God and the melodies of the world unfold as relational partners, seeking among the wreckage of tragedies and sorrows, the most intense harmony possible in our wide, welcoming universe.

Mrs. Whitehead and
the Bejeweled Universe

Every time we move, or think, we disturb the whole universe.

–Richard Lubbock

Funny how the world's most provocative ideas often appear to be wholly original, bearing no homage to past influence.   But this is an illusion of great proportions.   Creation *ex nihilo* simply bears no relational reality.   Even the words of a short essay like this one were born out of an infinite array of experiences of my mind and emotions, love and pain, inspirations and revulsions, all too numerous to name, too interwoven and unconscious ever to delineate fully.   Like an artist with a full palette of colors, we create our moments, our sermons and essays, our poetry, and the trajectory of our morality out of the complexity of the past; and hopefully, too, with the influence of the luminous souls we meet on our path.

And, to be honest, most of these souls are a mystery to us—unknown, unnamed, unsung.   But then one day you look in the rear-view mirror of influence and catch a glimpse of someone so surprising and unexpected that you slam on your breaks with excitement, causing a mental traffic pile-up.

This happened to me.   I was innocently re-reading the preface of one the most influential books in my own life, Alfred North Whitehead's classic, *Adventures of Ideas*—a predictable preface as prefaces go—nothing to write home about.   And then, without warning . . .

WHAM! The last sentence of the preface made me slam on my breaks. My cat, Monet, who was reading alongside me, nearly jumped sky-high.

And here's why all the commotion: Whitehead gave tribute to someone in the last sentence in an unexpected way—someone who influenced his ideas, *fundamentally*. Of course great philosophers have great influences: other philosophers of course. Not to mention education, culture, and experiences both tragic and beautiful. I would not have blinked an eye if he had listed these influences. But in the very last sentence to the preface to *Adventure of Ideas*, he writes: "I am indebted to my wife for many ideas fundamental to the discussion . . ."46

This is nothing short of astonishing, given the time period. Keep in mind, this is not a contemporary book. A. N. Whitehead (1861-1947) was a product of Victorian England, and the book was published in 1933—hardly a heyday for feminist philosophers. In those days, middle-class women were viewed more like my cat: the most important thing in the house, but doing nothing. And certainly not thinking big thoughts about the universe. They simply supported the men who did the thinking. But Whitehead did not thank Mrs. Whitehead as you would expect: not for her support and encouragement; nor for organizing the household so he could think and write; not even for her patience and long-suffering.

No.   He thanked her for her ideas—ideas *fundamental* to his own thinking.

Well then, so should I thank her, for now Mrs. Whitehead—*née* Evelyn Willoughby Wade—is no longer among the murky mass of influences that have created who I am and how I have lived my life. She has a name!

And not only that. After this bombshell in the preface to *Adventures of Ideas*, I scoured my library and the internet for more on Mrs. Whitehead while my cat, Monet, sat patiently and supportively alongside me (I still can't thank him for his ideas). Soon, I began to form a silhouette of the woman who so *fundamentally* influenced the great philosopher and mathematician.

It seems that this was not the only time Alfred mentioned Evelyn's influence. In 1941 A. N. Whitehead's *Autobiographical Notes* were published. In it Whitehead wrote:

> In December, 1890 my marriage with Evelyn Willoughby Wade took place. The effect of my wife upon my outlook on the world has been so fundamental that it must be mentioned as an essential factor in my philosophic output. . . . Her vivid life has taught me that beauty, moral and aesthetic, is the aim of existence; and that kindness, and love, and artistic satisfaction are among its modes of attainment.[47]

Note that word "fundamental" popping up again. She was no ornament; Evelyn had ideas. For this reason, Whitehead also said, "By myself I am only one more professor, but with Evelyn I am first-rate."[48]

Whitehead's wife was an Irish woman raised in France and saddled with a mouthful of names: Evelyn Ada Maude Rice Willoughby Wade. But what of her intellectual and artistic influences before meeting Alfred? How did she come to embrace ideas shot through with beauty and aesthetics and morality? Was she a saint or did she yell at rude store clerks? It would be nice to know these things because she is an intricate part of my intellectual heritage, and perhaps yours, too.

And then I came across this delicious tidbit from Richard Lubbock's iconic essay "Alfred North Whitehead—Philosopher for the Muddleheaded":[49] Evelyn Wade, says Lubbock, was "a high spirited, convent-educated daughter of an army officer. Whitehead family gossip reports that she once horsewhipped a man."

And it gets better . . .

Victor Lowe's biography of Whitehead reveals that Evelyn had a "low opinion" of her mother-in-law and that if strong-willed Evelyn failed to get her way in a marital clash, she would fall to her sofa with a pseudo-heart attack. Victor Lowe comments, "She was a sofa lady who always had just enough strength to be wonderful."[50]

You just have to love her. Alfred certainly did.

Whitehead was a philosopher before his time, so is it any wonder that he understood the significance of a woman's insight in a time when women like Evelyn were normally credited with nothing beyond their ability to have children, their physical beauty, and their charity work? Whitehead joyfully "prehended" that feminine philosophical voice as one of the, yes, *fundamental* influences in his thought. For those of us influenced by Whitehead's philosophy, Evelyn Willoughby Wade was a luminous part of it, without which Whitehead would not be Whitehead and we would not be We.

But this is Whitehead's philosophy all-over. Everything influences everything else so much that, as Richard Lubbock sums up Whitehead's cosmology with these brilliant words, "Every time we move, or think, we disturb the whole universe."

I am now looking at famous people differently, as conglomerates of other people who might be invisible to the world—but never, according to Whitehead's philosophy, to God and to the universe. There, in the beautiful mind of God, all is clear and shining and eternal and influential. In fact, Whitehead's world is very much like Indra's Net of Jewels from Hua-Yen Buddhism—a glittering cosmic net of jewels, each reflecting all the other jewels in the universe. We are, none of us, just individuals but are comprised of the reflections of every other jewel in the cosmos of influences. And that includes the jewels that are trees and stars and cats and whales—and divinity, too: the whole "Ten Thousand Things."

So, thank you, Mrs. Whitehead. Thank you for your brilliance in the cosmos of jewels, and for the fainting sofa that kept you human (not to mention the horsewhip). Thank you, thank you. Just, thank you.

S-I-Z-I-N-G Up

Our souls grow wide in gratitude and awe when we contemplate the sheer magnitude of influences that make up who we are. Not only do we create ourselves out of this vast array of mostly unknown influences, but we, in turn, quietly and unconsciously influence others—for good or ill. We help to fatten or impoverish the souls of the others by the choices we make. Even when we think we make no imprint on the world or have no real significance in the scheme of things, we do. For the fact is, we live in a bejeweled universe where everything reflects and everything connects.

The Glad Game Revisited

Think of all the beauty still left around you and be happy.
—Anne Frank

And most generally there is something about everything that you can be glad about, if you keep hunting long enough to find it.
—Eleanor H. Porter

Children are the best philosophers. Take the fictional Pollyanna. Oh, I know. Pollyanna is an odd subject for sophisticated readers, and it may be especially shocking to think of her as a "philosopher." After all, the very name of Pollyanna annoys, rankles, frequently inducing spontaneous winces, as it's nearly always used in a pejorative way. To be called "a Pollyanna" is to be called a naïvely cheerful person who wears rose-colored glasses and would not see reality if it bit her on the nose. No one wants to be called "a Pollyanna."

Years ago, as a young woman seeking acceptance with the intellectual sophisticates in my university's philosophy club—of which I served as president—I knew that to be accused of being "a Pollyanna" would rate as the worst possible insult. I'd seen it happen to fellow philosophers once or twice, so I took precautions: I wore black and tried hard to quit smiling so much in an effort to appear more anguished and "Existential" around my fellow grad students. Naturally, I shied away from *Pollyanna*, the book, a classic children's work, and would not be caught dead at the cinema watching the movie version—even though I was tempted. Instead, I dutifully attended those bleak art films directed by the Swedish existentialist Ingmar Bergman and left the theater wondering if life was, indeed, worth living.

Years later, after breaking down and secretly reading the book, I completely changed my opinion of Pollyanna. Turns out, I really did miss out on something. And now, in light of Fat Soul philosophy, I would like to clear Pollyanna's name—and even dare to suggest that she has something of great value to offer, especially when life looks as bleak as a Bergman film.

Pollyanna Was No Pollyanna

What I mean is that the actual character of Pollyanna—not her distortion, but the little girl who lives in Eleanor Porter's 1913 children's novel—simply wanted to promote a single idea: finding something to be "glad" about in any bad situation. But she did this without rose-colored glasses. At no point did she diminish, gloss over, or underrate the sadness or loss or tragedy of the situation. She knew and felt the distress of grief and loneliness at a young age. She cried as any child would. And through her sorrow, she became a compassionate child, actively participating in helping others, from a dog to an orphan boy. She did not embrace a helpless attitude, but rather a way of transforming her sadness. It's really quite sophisticated after all.

Today, I often hear the sunny philosophy of "It's all good," or "Everything has a reason." I wince at these blithe (but no doubt well-meaning) clichés, and so would Pollyanna. Such a philosophy of life would be foreign to Pollyanna—and to children in general. These sayings are, in essence, what we have always heard in some quarters of religion: "It must be God's will." If this is true, that everything is as it should be, there's not much need for compassion or active work in the world.

Whether speaking of God or a vague notion of the universe, the "all is good/there's a reason for everything" philosophy implies there is some all-controlling power out there that determines the scheme of things—that this bad event is part of a larger purpose or a "lesson" or "test." Many find this comforting—for about fifteen minutes. It breaks down quickly when we push the logic and begin to question the morality of God: What kind of God would teach lessons by way of unbearable suffering? What kind of a grand scheme could justify a child's suffering, mass murder, or genocide? This kind of God sounds a bit Machiavellian to me, and at the very least, psychopathic.

Fat Soul philosophy would say that all is *not* good. The melting of Arctic glaciers at an alarming rate is not good; poverty is not good; cancer is not good. There is no reason or higher purpose for these bad things. That's not how the universe works.

The Poet of the World

A Fat Soul kind of world is a relational world, where there is no one all-controlling power determining how the universe goes. We live in a world of flow, where chaos and randomness exist alongside goodness and beauty. Fat Soul spirituality aligns with process theologians who say that God is a loving, empowering Presence residing in every flowing moment of our lives. God feels the world, grieves with the world, and urges the world toward transformation—like an artist, a poet, a visionary dreamer. "God is the poet of the world, with tender patience leading it by his vision of truth, beauty, and goodness," says Whitehead.[51]

The Poet of the world desires to create beauty in the world, even out of the random chaos and violence that we witness on a daily basis. But we need to help God. We are part of God's poem. We make a difference in how the words are written in the world. That's what gives life meaning.

The Glad Game

When Pollyanna was a small child, she lost her mother, leaving only her father, a nearly destitute pastor of a missionary church. One day, Pollyanna's father sent a request to the missionary society for a doll for his daughter. Pollyanna was ecstatic to think of having a doll to love, but when the barrel came, it was not a doll. They sent a pair of crutches instead, with a note saying there were no dolls available, but perhaps the crutches would help someone. Pollyanna was naturally upset, and it was then her father taught her how to play The Glad Game.

Her father believed that God meant us to be glad, that we were to "rejoice and be glad." He challenged Pollyanna to find something about the situation to be glad about. It seemed impossible, until she realized that she could be glad that she *did not need* the crutches! Her sorrow was transformed, and thus began her child-like passion for finding something to be glad about in every circumstance, no matter how bad it got.

And it did get worse. Her father died and she was carted off to live with an aunt who did not want her, but felt it her duty to take in the child. Nevertheless, Pollyanna continued to play The Glad Game, even while she experienced rejection, discomfort, loneliness, and grief. She taught others in the community how to play—friends, adults, strangers—transforming their lives, too. She even wore down her crusty, cynical aunt, who, like us, was highly annoyed with Pollyanna's gladness.

Soul-Stretching Gratitude

The Glad Game falls under the larger umbrella of gratitude, but is specific to difficult times. It's easy to be grateful for the beauty we see, the goodness we know, and the people we love. But when things go badly, we must stretch the soul, sometimes to the limit. If we follow Pollyanna's childhood wisdom, we can be grateful, *not* for the accident or the disease or the sorry state of the world, but rather, for something within these things that challenges us toward truth, beauty, and goodness. That Something is the Poet of the world, who challenges us in every situation to gather up the ashes so the Phoenix can rise.

When the Worst Happens

Anne Frank was another child who refused to allow her lively spirit to be crushed by circumstances, but she was not a fictional character. Anne was real. We feel her realness while reading each unvarnished entry of her young teenage diary. She was naturally cheerful and hopeful, yet with an acute understanding of the very real evil and terror just outside her hiding place during the dark days of the Holocaust. As each entry date moves closer to August 4, 1944, we know what she does not know, and it breaks our hearts.

There is nothing good, true, or beautiful about what happened to Anne Frank on that August day, after two years of hiding and writing and hoping. The Nazis, having been tipped off, came and swept her away, along with all her youthful hopes and dreams of growing up. It is an evil beyond comprehension; the whole universe—the very Soul of the world—groaned in sorrow on that day, as with all the atrocities of that period. And yet, out of this horror arose the Phoenix: her diary left behind—saved by the courageous Miep Gies, who gathered up the scattered pages like ashes.

Anne had hoped to become a great writer and even to be read after her death. For this one thing we can be glad, as she would be glad: Her diary, her testament to goodness in the universe—her spirit—lives on.

The Challenge of the Game

So then, all is not good, but goodness can be resurrected and re-created into new forms of beauty, even if tinged with tragedy. As Whitehead says, "The Adventure of the Universe starts with a dream and reaps tragic beauty."[52]

Within everything, no matter how tragic, there is the possibility for something good, and it is up to us to find it, nurture it, and use it as the raw material for something new. And with each new challenge the soul grows larger, the mind grows wiser, and we learn to see and respond to the world differently.

But it doesn't happen automatically. It takes practice and courage and a belief in goodness, truth, and beauty. As with Miep Gies, who, after the Nazis came, gathered up among the wreckage the scattered pages of Anne Frank's diary, so we too can gather up scattered pieces of hope that have been left among the ruins and offer them back to the world in a new form. This is what the Poet of the world does; this is what we are called to do.

In the world of process theology, we call this "creative transformation"; in Pollyanna's world, it is called The Glad Game. Like all games, The Glad Game is not passive; it asks us to do something—to make a choice—and we get better with practice. It is a kind of spiritual discipline. Even small, irritating events and obstacles can serve as practice, which then prepares us for the tougher matches ahead. We simply train our minds to ask: *Even though this happened, what can I find to be glad about? How can I help God transform this situation? How can I be part of God's poem?*

The game stimulates our mind, our creativity, and our moral courage in the search for a gem of gladness in the midst of what might be grim reality. Children have a special sensitivity for such things, and we need to listen to them. They can help us avoid the soul-impoverishing extremes of giving in to the darkness, or pretending that nothing is really wrong. Children are the best philosophers.

S-I-Z-I-N-G Up

The poet Jack Gilbert once said, "We must have the stubbornness to accept our gladness in the ruthless furnace of this world."[53] Learning to play The Glad Game can help. If we can stretch our souls to the limit on bad days in order to discover something worth nurturing—

something of beauty—then we have, indeed, learned to be poets of our own lives. Pollyanna's philosophy is one that we adults would be wise to return to—once we give up our need to be morbidly depressed like everybody else. So, go ahead and dare to be "a Pollyanna." We are never too old or too sophisticated to play The Glad Game.

Malala's Monumental Soul

*When I was young I used to listen to other people
and to try and understand what they thought and
where they were coming from. I listened and
didn't speak.*

—Malala Yousafzai

Just when we thought that the moral courage of
Gandhi and Martin Luther King, Jr. and Cesar Chavez
and Rosa Parks was a thing of the past, the world
surprises us with a goddess of goodness: Malala
Yousafzai. The young Pakistani Nobel Peace Prize
winner, who survived a brutal shooting by the Taliban for
daring to be educated, stands as a model of moral
courage for our time. But what makes Malala tick? Why
doesn't she cower in the corner in fear for her life? Why
does she put herself out there, over and over, preaching
education for girls, knowing full well that she stands
squarely in the cross hairs of Taliban hatred?

Perhaps the answer lies partly in her faith. "Islam
means peace," Malala reminds us. It seems that Malala's
God is the polar opposite from the God of the Taliban. In
a BBC interview with Andrew Marr[54], she says of the
Taliban, "They were killing people for tiny issues like
dancing or not being dressed properly. They thought that
God is very conservative, God is very tiny." She says that
at judgment time, the Taliban God would ask about how
one is dressed or the length of one's beard before
ushering one into heaven. But she says no. God is more
concerned about character, about kindness, about how
we treat each other. Malala's God is a big-souled God

with room for diversity—a God who values justice and kindness and the power of education. Learning expands the mind, the soul, the psyche—whatever you call it. It makes us bigger. Learning calls for courage to move out beyond the impoverishment of tiny values, tiny ideas, and even a tiny God. Malala believes in the Bigness that an educated life offers, and lives it at the risk of her own safety for the sake of all girls and women who live tiny, windowless lives in patriarchal worlds where power lies in the hands of a few.

From a Fat Soul perspective, we might say that courage—moral courage—comes from a divine place within each moment of self-creation. That is, against the heavy weight of fear or revenge—natural, human feelings—Malala is responding to something rare and beautiful and divine, what Whitehead calls "the initial aim of God." That is, among all the possibilities for self-creation, Malala is responding to a divine lure: a lure toward the teleology of Beauty in the world, a lure toward bigness, toward intense harmonies made up of diverse people, religions, and cultures. It is a lure to rise above evil itself to fulfill her own special calling in life. Her mission for girls' education is born of her values, her Islamic faith, her experience of personal freedom through learning, and her well-honed skill of listening. Is it any wonder she is an inspiration to people all over the world?

I used to teach girls Malaya's age, and she reminds me of that refreshing idealism in the eyes of teenagers, that natural passion characteristic of youth. Some youth take those ideals into self-destructive violence as we witnessed at the Boston Marathon. But others like Malala are attune to something much wiser and higher and bigger. She is a model for Islam, a model of relational/persuasive power over unilateral/coercive power, and a picture of what moral courage looks like.

S-I-Z-I-N-G Up

We live in a world of violent religious fundamentalism, which sears the fabric of all goodness in the
world. But then there arises out of the darkness a bright
new star, youthful and fresh and healing. Malala is a
large and luminous and listening soul who reminds us of
that underlying Goodness that pervades the world. She
reminds us, too, of the soul-expanding power of
education to combat the small, mean, soul-impoverished
world of fundamentalism. Malala inspires us to expand
our souls not only with books and knowledge, but with
courage—active courage—in the face of all that is evil. We
can take heart when we need to stand up for what is right
and good and true; we can simply think of Malala and her
monumental courage on behalf of woman and education
and peace. Malala Yousafzai wins the Fat Soul
International Award for simply being Awesome.

Lennon/McCartney and the Virtues of Edginess

In a healthy spiritual life, it is important to be alienated as well as at home, to be troubled as well as peaceful, to be angry as well as satisfied.
—Jay McDaniel

Growing up with the Beatles was growing up with magic. All else in the world may have been falling apart at the seams, especially in Vietnam, but the Beatles were there—mixed up like the rest of us—illuminating our lives with their magical presence: a burst of novelty, a rush of feeling, a cultural bond. While they reveled in their rebellious role as cultural iconoclasts, we Baby Boomers feel like we're going home to a solid and true place when we hear their songs today.

The Beatles spanned and defined the Sixties. Those of us who filled our ears and imaginations and youthful yearnings with *Rubber Soul* and *Sgt. Pepper's Lonely Hearts Club Band* came to understand early on that the Lennon/McCartney writing team possessed a genius that was not privy to them as individuals, but only as artistic collaborators. They worked as two halves of a whole—an uneasy whole, a dynamic, often competitive and fractious whole, but still, a brilliant collaboration that survived the Sixties, just. Even their later solo albums were a collaboration in a sense, as by that time they had so deeply contributed to each other's musical evolution.

As a Fat Soul philosopher, it's hard not to see a little metaphysical magic going on, too. Part of this is disturbing: the Lennon part. John Lennon disturbed—

he was born to disturb. For most of his life, he was a rude, crude, and severely angry guy by his own account, with mega abandonment issues that eventuated into hard drugs and even "primal scream" therapy. John was the quintessential rebel who craved novelty to an addictive degree, reaping angst in equal measure. But there is something excoriatingly truthful about John Lennon—an edginess and absurdity and outrage that is life, or at least part of it.

In contrast to Lennon's gritty edge, we have Paul McCartney, a warm, likeable Liverpudlian lad, with large angelic eyes and two feet solidly on the ground—at least most of the time, at least until his boyhood chum, John Lennon, persuaded him to jump over the wall of the factory where he held a steady paying job, and go for it. Paul was the "light" who gave us "Yesterday" and "Let It Be" and "Blackbird," and all the tender songs that made us catch our breath. And yet, even his most lovely and deceptively simple piece, "Blackbird," possesses a subtle edginess and complexity: the blackbird is a metaphor for a black woman facing oppression of that era. Musically there are several changes of time signature and a Bach-like complexity, all of which adds interest.

Paul's melodic musical voice was enhanced by John's gritty edge; John's penchant for discord found harmony in Paul's gift for melody. They played off one another and needed each other to create lasting works of art in the pop world. Perhaps that's why, throughout their stormy relationship—nearly seared in half when the Beatles broke up—they remained devoted to one another. Without Paul, John would have probably crashed and burned. And yet, without John, Paul might have never found that edge, that strand of the absurd that took him into the realm of genius. They needed each other, two contrasting personalities meeting, bumping up against each other, each drawing out what the other needed to create one of the most brilliant songwriting teams in history.

Like Paul, we all need a bit of edginess in our lives to discover the depths of what Whitehead would call beauty. For Whitehead, beauty is not perfect harmony. He would call that "anesthesia." Anesthesia is peace without much truth, harmony without much depth. Anesthesia is a trivial sort of harmony, like a high school clique that excludes the nerds and other uncool kids, or a church which excludes gays, or a religion which believes it is the only truth in the world. Anesthesia is a colorless world of sameness and safety and closed doors. Anesthesia is harmonious all right, but it is not beautiful.

Real beauty relishes collaborations of opposites, chiaroscuro-like contrasts, and the right amount of edginess to be solid and true and lasting. Bach knew this secret, and so did Stravinsky and Mozart and Dave Brubeck and every other great composer who understands the power of suspension, a change of key or time signature, syncopation, or the odd dissonant chord at the right moment in time. Lennon and McCartney knew this secret intuitively, and it separated them from most of the rock bands of the time.

Professor and musician Jay McDaniel, who created the popular website *Jesus, Jazz, and Buddhism*, understands this delicate balance in music and in life. He is what I would call an "idea artist," who can take an abstract idea and sculpt endlessly fresh configurations and novel relationships out of it—and still be true to the idea. He's like a jazz artist, constantly improvising on a given chord structure. And, like all artists, he is edgy, too. He offers discordant notes for the sake of beauty. For example, he dares to talk about God as not just light, but darkness, too—the "alienated side of God," which is especially clear in the biblical passages where God is angry at injustice and "moved to pity by the sufferings of the outcasts, the marginalized, the forsaken, and the forgotten." Jay calls this the "kick-ass" side of God.[55]

But of course, God is not edgy in a bad way, an evil way, an irresponsible way. God does not go in for hard drugs and rudeness and iconoclastic madness like the youthful Lennon—but sometimes, I do think I hear a Primal Scream searing through the universe . . .

The edginess of God is a kind of Divine Discontent, and why Jay says, "The point is that, in a healthy spiritual life, it is important to be alienated as well as at home, to be troubled as well as peaceful, to be angry as well as satisfied."[56]

So, taking a riff from Jay McDaniel, I too, feel the freedom to say that God is a bit crazy, a bit dark, a bit "kick ass." An empathetic God has to be, for the world is suffering and filled with injustice. A God who doesn't feel the darkness and lure us to do something about it—kick a little ass—is not a beautiful God.

And God is beautiful. I believe that. Maybe that's why, in my seasoned years, I'm drawn back in time to my favorite three Bs: Bach, Brubeck, and the Beatles. And maybe it's why I feel both peaceful and discontent at the same time—and know that it's okay. In fact, it's beautiful.

S-I-Z-I-N-G Up

Those of us who are by nature more Paul McCartney than John Lennon can, when necessary, stretch our souls toward the edgy for the sake of the world. We may need to speak up, protest, or be the counter-cultural gadfly in a situation without soul, without justice, without mercy. To create more soul in soulless situations, we may need to take off our kid gloves and tap into our "kick ass" side.

Dave Brubeck: Theology in 5/4 Time

The art of progress is to preserve order amid change, and to preserve change amid order. Life refuses to be embalmed alive.
—Alfred North Whitehead

You don't have to love hardcore jazz to love Dave Brubeck. One of the few jazz geniuses to cross over to the mainstream without compromising his musical integrity, he enchanted—and continues to enchant—a wide swath of music lovers. As a young saxophonist in a high school jazz band in the early Seventies, I was one of the beguiled, finding special inspiration in Brubeck's cool-as-a-cucumber sax player, Paul Desmond. Today, I don't play the saxophone very often, but I do play Brubeck, for his music helps me imagine a truly creative approach to life, one that constantly challenges the status quo without forsaking it altogether—revolution, yes, but not bloody revolution. Change amid order. Zest amid harmony. It speaks of a Whiteheadian view of the world, a process-relational world, a daringly beautiful world of "creative transformation."

A Syncopated Sort of a Life (and Death)

David Warren "Dave" Brubeck (December 6, 1920-December 5, 2012) died one day before his 92nd birthday. One day! Maybe he planned it that way, for it is surely a syncopated way to die. Not quite on the beat.

And that's what we love about him.

"Take Five," his masterpiece single from the album *Time Out* (1959), broke through all the known boundaries of jazz of the time by simply adding an extra beat to the measure. Four beats turned into five. Five beats? Oh, come on. Who can dance to that? Well, you don't have to dance to it; just feel it, and let it pick you up and hurdle you through the door of "what is" into that new musical dimension called "what can be." This is what Brubeck did for his art form: he stretched out jazz like it was warm taffy—not to the breaking point, but well beyond the known boundaries. With time signatures pushed beyond their comfort zones, we witness one of those historic musical moments when order meets zest, when jazz refuses to be embalmed in established forms.

An Excellent Paradox

The *Atlantic* calls his ability to reinvent jazz rhythms while still being true to tradition "an excellent paradox."[57] Excellent, indeed. And like all excellent paradoxes, it works somehow, creating yet a new form of jazz that then becomes the tradition for the next paradox to strike. In this way, Brubeck opened the door to radically new jazz rhythms just as, say, Einstein opened the relativity door leading to quantum physics. Somebody had to do it, and Brubeck had the courage, the genius, or at least enough mischief to give in to the witty muse of 5/4 time—not to mention 9/8 time.

So, Brubeck's new rhythms became like the fifth dimension in jazz, dismantling our musical pre-conceptions and thrusting us forward to imagine things unheard of—like walking on the moon. It feels happy, too, listening—or singing—in 5/4 time. It never ceases to feel a bit startling, catching one off balance, like a lover going out the door and suddenly turning back for one last kiss.

But how does such a thing happen? What goads the imagination toward novelty, the kind which adds such richness to the world? Process theology would say that such novelty comes from God, the very Soul of the world, the ultimate, organizing source of not only order, but things-not-yet. And the more we open our minds to new worlds and new ways of thinking, the more likely we are to pick from the fresh possibilities ripening in the divine mind, awaiting those who dare to imagine.

Sometimes, it's just a matter of putting ourselves in a new situation and being fully aware and alive in the moment. This very thing happened to Dave Brubeck. Joshua Rothman from *The New Yorker* explains: "In the nineteen-fifties, the U.S. State Department cultivated a group of 'jazz ambassadors,' whom they would send on tour around the world to demonstrate the overwhelming coolness of American culture. In 1958, they sent the Dave Brubeck Quartet to East Germany, Poland, Turkey, Afghanistan, India, Sri Lanka, Iran, and Iraq."[58]

Rothman says that it was in Istanbul that Brubeck became fascinated with the unusual rhythms and exotic syncopations of street musicians. They were playing in an oddly alluring 9/8 time—nine eighth notes per measure (unheard of to Western ears!)—and that was just the beginning. That was the spark that ignited a jazz revolution. In 1959, when he returned from his world tour, his quartet recorded *Time Out*, where he not only introduces 5/4 time (five quarter notes per measure) in "Take Five," but also the ultra-exotic 9/8 time in "Blue Rondo a la Turk."

The Source of Life-Enriching Novelty

As with many creative people, Brubeck was a spiritual person who also wrote sacred music, such as one of my favorite Christmas hymns, "God's Love Made Visible." (Of course, it is in 5/4 time—would we want it any other way?) Is it any wonder that spirituality—though not always orthodox—and creativity tend to coincide? But then, if God is the source of life-enriching novelty, it begins to make sense.

Whitehead believed that Creativity is the most real thing about the universe. Some people are especially gifted in their awareness of novel ideas, but we can all live like a jazz artist if we are aware of this deep, loving, divine reality always beckoning us toward freshness.

Creativity—our freedom to choose—does not necessarily mean we will choose what is good or beautiful or even novel. Change is not always called for and not always good—yes, sometimes we need to preserve order amid change—but our choices are always fresh and they always matter to the universe and to God. Whether it is a radical departure or steady-as-she-goes, the unleashing of whatever is good and true and beautiful within our souls is a creative act that process thinkers call "creative transformation."

The John Cobb of Jazz

But how do moments of high novelty ever really get off the ground when life is so weighted down by the heaviness of the past—the status quo? Whitehead believed that reality is not as solid and heavy and unforgiving as we think. He believed reality is made up of energy events or "occasions of experience," much like musical vibrations. These occasions of experience or vibrations tend to create things we see like pianos and saxophones and horned-rimmed glasses. Whitehead calls this tendency the "historic route of occasions." Such historic routes of energy events also create what we hear or feel or under-stand as tradition—like religious tradition or musical tradition. We can say, then, that the tradition of jazz *before* Brubeck had a particular historic route. It was dominated by certain ideas and sounds that did not include wild, far-out time signatures.

But in the late 1950s, the jazz tradition—its particular historic route of occasions—needed some infusion of freshness, for it was getting a bit stale, stifling, unimaginative, i.e., status quo. Then one day, the tradition of American jazz meets a radically fresh occasion, one from yet another historic route of occasions, a wholly different tradition from the streets of Istanbul. A light goes on in Brubeck's musical mind—an "aha!" moment. This fresh idea, this new occasion of experience that leaps from the exotic Turkish music and lands in the receptive mind of Brubeck, is the lure of God, what Whitehead calls the "initial aim," for an entirely new creation.

In this new creation, the old way of jazz is not abandoned; rather, the old is enriched and intensified. This new thing—American jazz braving discombobulating time signatures—becomes an instance of creative transformation. Jazz, then, becomes an intensely fresh, living, breathing, route of occasions that will, in its turn, become an historic route in need of further infusions of novelty.

Given this, I think Dave Brubeck qualifies as a musical process theologian—perhaps the "John Cobb of Jazz." And, in the same way, John Cobb could be thought of as the "Dave Brubeck of Theology."

It's not a bad comparison. In the mid-twentieth century, while Brubeck was taking jazz beyond its borders of tradition, John Cobb was busy taking theology in a similar direction of originality. Cobb opened up a creative way for theologians—and thoughtful people in general—to think about God outside the stifling theological box of 4/4 time. He used the occasion of Whitehead's and Hartshorne's influence to infuse theology's past historic route with a fresh understanding of God and world. And it has an entirely fresh rhythm.

This view of God, the process view, happens to be very much like a jazz musician: always improvising in the world-as-it-is with some new creative lure for what might be—what *can* be. A relational God may be limited by the freedom inherent in the world, but never boxed in by 4/4 time. Oh, no. This God believes in jazz.

S-I-Z-I-N-G Up

Fat Souls are grounded in the wisdom of the past without being embalmed by the past. They move, they groove, they improvise—and sometimes they revolutionize. Such is the rhythm of Fat Soul.

Part Four

The S-I-Z-E of Hope

The Quaking and Breaking of Everything

Here is the world. Beautiful and terrible things will happen. Don't be afraid.
—Frederick Buechner

I do not believe in the up there/out there bully in the sky. I would much rather celebrate the cosmic companion who is creating a universe in which I, and the rest of creation, am invited toward cosmos, connection, justice and love.
—Rabbi Bradley Artson

Many waters cannot quench love, neither can floods drown it.
—The Song of Solomon 8:7

Once a year, during the rainy season on the wild and beautiful coast in Ecuador, everything suddenly breaks—trees and foundations and habitats and earth. It is the yearly quaking and breaking that brings about a rush of mud and timber down the rivers from the distant, mysterious, mist-covered mountains.

Where we live, on the north central coast, the Jama River flows down and out into the Pacific Ocean, lavishly spreading out, surrendering to the wide, welcoming sea, as if finally reaching nirvana. But the river's peace can be suddenly and brutally ruptured. In a single day, hundreds of rootless trees rush down the river, fall helplessly into the battering chaos of the tide, and finally succumb to their final resting place on the beach.

The volcanic sandy beach, pristine and empty one day, becomes nature's graveyard the next. This sudden appearance of massive timber makes one wonder at the brutal force of the water—how it could unearth whole, living, thriving trees from their homes on the banks of peaceful rivers and streams. Like corpses strewn about without dignity on a battlefield, the fallen, battered trees tell of something unimaginable, of a violence that makes the blood run cold.

Here Is the World . . .

The metaphor opens up like a river to the sea of all humanity, everywhere. We may not be besieged by war, but nevertheless we are besieged. We, like trees, are products of nature. So, too, we are often ravaged by nature's force, by death and loss and illness. Here is the world: the sudden death of a loved one—one day the world is sunny, the next, all is lost. If we live long enough and deep enough, at some point in life, we will experience a quaking and breaking of everything we considered solid and sure. Simply growing up means experiencing the quaking and breaking from one stage of development to another, until we reach maturity. Growing old, with its gradual losses, feels like one felled tree after another. And in the middle, between youth and old age, the quaking and breaking continues.

When I moved to a foreign country in 2011, the world seemed to be pulled out from under me: identity, security—everything uprooted. This very quaking and breaking defines huge chunks of our existence.

Here is the world, at least if we live deeply and vibrantly and dare to put down roots somewhere. We are meant to plant within ourselves many solid green trees that grow deep and tall and feel the shimmering of wind in their leaves. But not all of it stays put. Surging water flows and knocks us off our feet—it is inevitable.

Beautiful and Terrible Things Will Happen . . .

So the question, then, after the quaking and breaking subsides, is this: can we ever find solid ground again—a sense of reassurance that something is solid somewhere? The bleached, smooth corpses of trees, even in their stark demise, seem to answer in the affirmative. Of course time, nature's natural remedy, comes into play. Eventually the sand will cover up the mass of dead timber, or it will be caught by a tide in the full moon and be swept away to other shores. People will come and carry it off to build houses and fences. The shore will, with time, be cleared. But time does not always clear away the debris of pain and heartbreak, not all by itself.

After sitting for a while among the dead trees, I stood and stretched and looked up at the pillowy clouds and back to the mist-covered mountains in the distance, and then toward the wide sea. A flock of pelicans flew overhead on a mission to somewhere. And it occurred to me that one way through the quaking and breaking moments of life is simply to widen our vision. For it is only natural that when even a single tree is torn from its roots, we feel as though everything is lost; that this single brutality drowns out all other signs of life. Our eyes lock themselves firmly on the pain and injustice and waste of this beautiful tree, so that we soon identify with the pain, until finally, we *are* the pain.

But we can stretch out our awareness a bit—slowly at first—until, one day, something within us suddenly breaks loose and we can see it: the whole, wide spacious sky. *It is still there!* We turn around to see verdant hills and mountains made of solid rock. *They are still standing!* We look toward the endless gray-blue sea still pounding out its ancient rhythm onto a welcoming shore. *It is all still there!*

There is *more*, then, than this catastrophe, and given time, the More-ness of life can save us from petrifying pain. Perhaps the Buddhist idea of mindfulness can help us, for in meditation we learn to step back and observe the whole, to resist the urge to get caught up in the pain, and instead, care for the pain as a loving mother comforts a child. This very tender part of us, in process terms, can be seen as the tenderness of God. No matter what religious tradition we spring from, we all have this ability, for if we are spiritually inclined at all, we have within us a reservoir of deepness and wideness out of which flows fresh possibilities of seeing the whole and being reassured by the whole.

Don't Be Afraid . . .

When living in California, my husband and I always looked forward to Yom HaShoah services at Chapman University because of a man named Leon Leyson.[59] He passed away recently, and it felt as though a solid tree had been uprooted in our lives, for he was not only a friend, but a man who taught us about the More-ness of life. He was a Holocaust survivor, the youngest on Schindler's list, one of over 1,200 Jews Schindler saved. So when Leon lit the solemn yellow candle and told his story, it was a story that both chilled and reassured. He bore witness to great evil, yes, but he also bore witness to great courage and goodness, a stubborn root in the human spirit.

This stubborn goodness in certain people like Oskar Schindler reveals a stubborn goodness in the universe, a certain kind of power that process theologians call the loving, persuasive power of God. Hitler's form of power modeled itself on an omnipotent image of God, an almighty, controlling cosmic force, what Rabbi Artson so aptly calls "the bully in the sky" image of God. Leon Leyson spoke of another sort of power: the power of compassion and goodness and courage in an unlikely hero called Oskar Schindler. Here, too, is the world: Compassion speaks of God, and of a wide tenderness that embraces our fragile, terrible, beautiful world.

So, when all the quaking and breaking is over, we can rise from our grief, stretch, and look around for signs of the More-ness of life, for hints and glimpses of that stubborn, unquenchable goodness at the heart of the world, a compassion—a tender love—so deep and wide and high that it can never be drowned. For here is God, that "Cosmic Companion" who whispers to us: *Don't be afraid.*

S-I-Z-I-N-G Up

In Jay McDaniel's book *Living from the Center*, he says that when something terrible has happened, it can help "to go outside on a clear night and gaze into the dark and starlit sky in perfect silence. The sky and its stars can be a holy icon, an enfolding womb in which we feel small but included in a greater wholeness. The greater wholeness is God, the Open Space." He goes on to say that "faith is a trustful letting go, in which we open out into the divine mystery and feel included in a larger whole." It is a process, he says, of "going wide," a "movement of the soul, invisible to outsiders, in which the heart opens out in the Open Space and the Open Space wells up in the heart."[60] This is at the heart of Fat Soul healing. To expand our souls in the face of something terrible seems impossible, but if we can learn step by step to "go wide" into the spaciousness of God and trust in the Open Space, we will eventually find and enter that clear and starlit sky.

A Whole Universe of Stories

We are in the midst of seismic cultural change. In the old paradigm, priorities are shaped by a mechanistic worldview that privileges whatever can be numbered, measured, and weighed; human beings are pressured to adapt to the terms set by their own creations. Macroeconomics, geopolitics, and capital are glorified. . . . In the new paradigm, culture is given its true value. The movements of money and armies may receive close attention from politicians and media voices, but at ground-level, we care most about human stories, one life at a time.

–Arlene Goldbard

Growing up through the cracks of the broken worldview we call modernity are verdant shoots we call stories—human stories built of words and images and feelings and connected threads of subjective experience. We see them everywhere, not only in film and literature, but in the daily lives of regular people telling their own stories about where they come from and what makes them happy or sad, about people they love and animals that make them laugh or weep. About what makes life meaningful.

These are the messy, imperfect bursts of life that modernity views with suspicion. After all, stories lack "objectivity" and precision; they can't be tested and measured—or trusted. Unless stories can be marketed for big profits, they are devalued and walked over without a thought. But they just keep shooting up through the cracks—all these human stories on the internet, in faith communities, in murals and memoirs and songs—living, fresh, personal stories that don't quite jive with a mechanistic worldview.

And along with the spurting up of verdant stories comes a little cosmic irony. For all our modern advances, a sustainable future may depend on what we have left behind long ago: the stories and myths that birthed us into being. We need to replant ourselves in stories as we move into a new, organic stage of human consciousness— one that just might save the day in the eleventh hour of our questionable future on planet Earth.

Stories circle back to the past, to ancient peoples, storytellers and shamans who told their hair-raising and comedic tales of creation around warming fires—or painted their stories on damp, cool cave walls. Stories in sacred texts are like this, too. But sacred texts are old and cracked like cave paintings, and not many people pay attention to them anymore. But as constructive post-modernists—aka Fat Souls who dare to dream of a better world—we do pay attention. We have to. We need to read, listen, watch, and *feel* the stories all around us, for stories teach us about empathy and connect us to the world and to God and to God's body, the earth.

Stories make us larger.

All our stories—written, spoken, sung, painted, danced—come from way down deep, from an ancient place, an organic and healing place. In the beginning, our stories are the sparks flung out from the primordial fireball itself. Like our expanding universe, these are the ongoing stories of the world, of people and frogs and trees and floods and revolutions and love and war, and even species extinction. We need them—all of them, no matter how sad or how insignificant they may seem. For in an organic world, a process world, a Fat Soul kind of world, all stories matter.

Our stories matter because we live in a narrative universe. In a philosophy of organism, the worldview of Alfred North Whitehead, stories make up everything.

Stories begin with experience and are shot through with feeling. They inherit from the past and contribute to the future. They have a beginning, a middle, an ending; they become and perish, and yet live forevermore in the eternal unfolding of new stories. In this way stories are through and through organic, relational, always in process, and never quite finished. Even in God, Whitehead would say, tragic stories are creatively transformed from mere wreckage to "tragic Beauty." In this way, stories become another word for hope.

The entire universe consists of stories within stories within stories—within stories! As Jay McDaniel says, "People have their stories; animals have their stories; plants have their stories; the earth has its story; stars have their stories; and heaven has its story, too. Sometimes the stories are pleasant and sometimes painful. Often they are both and always they intersect. We are storied into existence by the stories of others."[61]

We could say that the world, instead of being made of "turtles all the way down," is made of stories all the way down. But if we think of stories as frameworks for human meaning, we can also say that stories go all the way up! A child's life is a story that finds meaning in the story of a family, which finds meaning in the story of community, which finds meaning in the story of global community, which finds meaning in the cosmological stories of the universe. Stories go all the way up to the sky and journey through the stars and planets and galaxies. We are storytellers; we are meaning-makers.

And so the ancient storytellers and shamans rise up within our collective memory, and we tell our stories of personal and communal and religious and cosmic experience. We see ourselves within the stories that are trees and stories that are rivers and stories that are lady bugs and stories that are seeds. We do this, as did our ancestors, because stories nurture meaning and ecological community and psychic wholeness. Each tiny story matters, for it is part of the larger cosmological story, each story adding to the beauty of God. Within this sacred universe of stories, we find our place among the stars and rocks and snowy egrets. We find something of beauty; we find our significance.

S-I-Z-I-N-G Up

Stories stretch out our souls with feeling, complexity, ambiguities, and finally, with what process thinkers call "creative transformation." Sometimes that transformation comes in the telling itself: we need to share our stories. We need to listen to the stories of others. Stories make us bigger. A soul filled with stories is a huge soul chock-full of not only grand themes, but of tiny details—the quotidian, the everyday. All of this makes us feel at home inside our grand and storied universe.

Novel Theology:
Our Unfolding Stories

[God] is the poet of world . . .
                    –Alfred North Whitehead

At the heart of the nature of things, there are always the dream of youth and the harvest of tragedy. The Adventure of the Universe starts with a dream and reaps tragic Beauty.
                    –Alfred North Whitehead

There is something to be said about the writer's old adage: Write the first draft with your heart, and the second with your head. This is especially true for improvisational writers like me. By improvisational writing, I mean something akin to the jazz artist who, out of the possibilities within a given chord progression, creates a spontaneous melody as she goes along. This is, technically speaking, the "organic" approach to writing. As both an essayist and novelist, my writing falls into this category, that is, taking a cue from a single thread of an idea and playing it out "as the spirit moves." If it gels into something coherent, the creative process wins. If not, it can be set aside or discarded. Essays work well this way, often needing only light editing. But the novel—an unwieldy cauldron of multiple personalities—is a whole other story.

Truth be told, the characters in my novels run the show, giving real meaning to the term "character-driven." (How I envy those who can plot every jot and tittle and stick to it! But, alas, my characters prove uncooperative.)

I work from a tentative outline, and yes, I lure my characters in that direction. But they do have a will of their own and a definite say-so in the plot. So I listen and write and let the narrative take its course, constantly readjusting my plot as events unfold. The end result is usually quite different from anything I imagined when I started.

And then comes the re-write . . .

Once the euphoria of the finished story subsides, reality sets in. Like all first-flush creations born of the enthusiastic heart, first drafts cry out for that second stage of creation, the brass tacks, the hard, analytic thinking. My characters, with their free-wheeling personalities, now have to take a backseat to the pesky realities of logical coherence, continuity, detail, and foreshadowing—not to mention the painful, gritty, mind-numbing work of copy editing. But there's no getting around it. Creativity must, in the end, give way to craft.

So, with a deep breath and copious amounts of tea, I take the novel as it is, and transform it into what it can be—much like the organic, improvisational world of process philosophy. Process theologian Marjorie Suchocki says that God "works with the world as it is in order to bring it to what it can be."[62] Thus, the entire artistic process of writing and re-writing can serve loosely as a metaphor for what Whitehead calls "creative trans-formation."

The process world of Alfred North Whitehead is a story unfolding in time with no pre-determined outcome. Many influences are at work in the writing, like strong-willed characters colliding against each other. And yet, every becoming moment of the story also includes a divine urge toward intense harmony. Whitehead calls this Beauty. In fact, the "poet of the world" lures us always and forever toward Beauty. The divine poet beckons and persuades and lures us forward with enticing possibilities, but can never strong-arm a character's action. So, in a sense, God works as the improvisational/organic writer works—not as an all-powerful tyrant over characters and plot, determining the outcome from the beginning, but rather as the poet of possibilities, luring the narrative into realms of richly contrasted Beauty.

When it comes to our individual stories—our personal stories within the cosmic story—we choose our own words. And not always with care. Bombarded by a plethora of influences all vying for a place on the page, we make our choices of nouns and verbs, characters and plot, metaphors and meaning, and hope for something close to a happy ending. But things happen. Is it any wonder that we find ourselves in constant need of revision? We ignore the divine lure toward Beauty on a daily basis, sometimes making a holy mess of things. Or, we simply write ourselves into a corner and don't know how to get out. And even when we do our best to write our stories on the dreams of youth, evil characters lurk among the pages and unforeseen tragedy dismantles our carefully constructed plot.

But thankfully there is always more to the story. God, Whitehead believed, is not only the lure toward Beauty, but the reaper of tragic Beauty when the story goes awry. This divine companion—the poet of the world—is our constant co-writer, who is able to take our flawed and fractured lives and re-imagine them into fresh metaphors of meaning. Just as words are alive and open to a thousand interpretations, so the past is alive and breathing, just waiting for a fresh word, an embrace of love, a divine imagination that can re-create out of the wreckage we have wrought.

S-I-Z-I-N-G Up

No, we cannot erase the actual facts of the story we have written with our lives—the past—but we can transform those facts into an ongoing story that can still be made beautiful. In fact, isn't that what we love most about stories—the redemption of flawed characters? In this way, no story is really set in stone. All can be redeemed; all can re-interpreted; all can be re-imagined and loved and forgiven and woven into the cosmic story that unfolds under a canopy of stars in a universe of glimmering possibilities.

When Things Fall Apart

I'm slipping. I'm slipping away like sand.
—Rainer Maria Rilke

Things fall apart. Every single day. All over the world. Like tidal waves, forces beyond our control can suddenly overtake us, drowning out all we thought was solid and true and forever. And when it's over (supposing we survive), there is that odd space of time when we just stand there, mute and still and unblinking—like marble statues—as if that will keep the tidal wave of emotion from breaching our psyches. But eventually, it does.

The Rock Garden

I live in a fishing village on the coast of Ecuador. Recently, we had an actual tidal wave, or rather, a devastating series of tidal waves that ravaged our village, bringing the ocean to our very doorstep—literally—with a force and brutality that wiped out our fragile beach, the only thing between us and what the poet Robinson Jeffers calls the great "Eye of the earth," the Pacific Ocean.[63]

During the onslaught of waves that took no prisoners, it was odd, the things I thought about. You would think I would have worried about our home, our neighbors' homes, the fishermen, their boats, the village itself—all the big things. But these were perhaps too big to take in, and so, in refuge, my thoughts turned to smaller things like my rock garden.

My Japanese rock garden—a simple *wabi-sabi* affair—is a basic spiral made up of the colorful, small rocks I have collected at low-tide. Rocks bring a sense of comfort and peace and connection to things past, and to eternity itself. The open-ended spiral shape of the rock garden represents the ongoingness of the garden, because it will, of course, grow through the years as I continue to collect rocks. That was the plan, anyway, a solid and hopeful plan.

But then the waves came, and despite our best human efforts to protect our property the sea surged in like an uninvited guest, ravenous and demanding, and worst of all, dispassionate. The massive waves crested and boomed against the shore, taking with it meters and meters of precious beach. The ocean surged toward us effortlessly, wrenching out palm trees from their roots and tossing them out to sea before turning back for more—tearing out huge chunks of land. Insatiate, the sea eventually found its way over and around the sandbags to our little house, claiming our yard, surging over everything in sight, including my *wabi-sabi* rock garden.

I knew the rock garden had been swept away, or at least torn apart—the smaller rocks dispersed, some of them now swimming in the very ocean that gave them to me in the first place. Despair began to wash over me. But when the water finally receded, there it was! There was my rock garden—covered with muck and mud and wood and trash—but it was intact, fully itself, unmoved, stubbornly just *there*. The hardy rocks looked back at me, sullied and sad, yes, but also with a kind of Zen-like equanimity about them.

The devastation to our village was massive, and more tidal waves—even worse—are expected later this year, putting not only houses and nest eggs in danger, but a whole way of life—the only known way of life—for the fishermen who have fished these equatorial waters for generations. We now live in a "disaster area." But how could this be? One day everything is fine, and the next, everything is falling apart. Just like that.

This is life, how it is for people all over the world who wake up to natural disaster or a devastating diagnosis or the failure of a business or the falling apart of a marriage. Buddhists tell us that life is suffering, and the more we deny this truth or try to gloss over it, the more we fall apart inside. So we look for something to ground us, to help us on the road to uncovering that equanimity of spirit that can lead to transformation.

For me, in this particular disaster, my grounding came through my rock garden. While clearing away the muck and mud from the rocks, it occurred to me that underneath our helplessness and anguish, there is something beautiful and solid and true, something open-ended and never-ending. Some call it God or simply Love. I call it both, for I believe that God is love.

Despair Transformed

Life can turn on a dime. It often does. Disaster washes over us as effortlessly and dispassionately as a tidal wave, and with it comes despair. Despair is part of life, but it does not have to drown us. We can use it to find the deep things, the covered up things, the solid and true things like love, like God, like our precious connection to the earth and sea. There are many treasures hidden under the waters of despair.

We are reminded, too, of our vulnerability in a world that is not solid or true or even trustworthy at times. Everything is changing constantly, and just when we start to settle in and get comfortable, the bottom drops out. The old sea god Poseidon humbles us without so much as an apology. We feel vulnerable and small in such a universe.

We have to be patient with despair because it takes time for the water and mud and muck to recede before we can see what is solid and true—and salvageable. There is much cleaning up to do. Our village has much to clean up, too, and much to think about as the tides keep taking and taking.

I do not believe there is anything about such destruction that is purposeful or "meant to be" or part of a divine plan. Like tidal waves, beautiful and terrible, our gorgeous world is also a brutal world—and terrible things happen in nature, too. The universe is not a great epic novel where all the tragic scenes have a purpose in the overall narrative. This is real life, where real tragedies drown-out real dreams and break real hearts, including the heart of God.

God Is in the Story

We are all writing the world together: you, me, the Pacific Ocean, and God. The future is not yet written. As process philosopher Bob Mesle often reminds us, **"the future does not exist."**[64]   We have to write the story together, word by word, sentence by sentence, chapter by chapter.   God is that Tender Presence that lures us toward transformation—the "poet of the world."   This God yearns for intense harmony within creation, and lures all creation toward that end which Whitehead calls "Beauty." But God is not all-controlling; poets and lovers never are. God feels the world completely, every part of it, and never gives up on it—or us. We, too, yearn for a beautiful ending, a just ending, a satisfying ending, and that gives us purpose in how and what we write. But the future is not yet written.

God is not an omnipotent Author of the Universe who permits suffering for the sake of a better story. That is not what we have. What we have is a Lover of the Universe who is part of the story itself, entangled in the messy chaos, suffering with those who suffer, daring to "reap tragic beauty" where the world leaves stark wreckage. This Cosmic Lover needs us and desires us— our prayers, our thoughts, our bodies, our intellect, even our anguish. For all is felt and transformed in the heart of God and offered back to the world in the form of freshness and hope.

God is in the story, in the earth. In us. This is not the old omnipotent deity "up there," but the God of the green earth and the blue sky and roaring sea and of eternal starry nights where despair and hope co-mingle. This is not the God who controls the tides, but the God

Underneath, who persists, quietly weaving tapestries out of the threads of tragedy. This is not the God of Destruction, but the God of Presence, the God of suffering, the God of transformation and healing, the "great companion who understands."

When the Worst Happens . . .

So, when the worst happens, when we are over-whelmed with tidal waves that break our world apart, we can know that underneath it all lies something persistent and beautiful and true and forever open-ended with possibility. Even if life itself should end, we are safe inside God's heart, that great cosmic womb in which nothing is ever lost: a heaven of transformation and healing. Like the spiraled rock garden, there is no closing off into despair—ever. There is movement, always movement toward freshness and novelty and transformation. That is the way of beauty, the way of love, the way of God in the world.

At least for now, my rock garden is spruced up and showing off its kaleidoscope of colors in the equatorial sunshine, reminding me that no matter what happens in the future, with the tides, the village, even with our home—still a hanging question mark—there is something beyond worry and despair. Something fresh. Call it Beauty, call it God, call it Love. I call it an open-ended God, a beautiful God, a suffering but solidly loving God: a Rock of Ages.

S-I-Z-I-N-G Up

When things fall apart, the soul naturally wants to shrink back in fear and anxiety and a sense of despair. It's only natural. But slowly, with time, we can learn to expand again, to take in the deep breath of faith in Something Solid—a beauty that does not wash away. The Soul of the world breathes new life and buoyancy into our own souls and we go on, timidly at first, but with increasing confidence. Through every experience of loss, we have at least this: the opportunity to gain a larger, more elastic, and resilient soul.

Our Ongoing Influence

Our thoughts, speech, and actions are our real continuation . . . it's possible to continue beautifully into the future . . . Nothing is lost.
—Thich Nhat Hanh

God's nature . . . is that of a tender care that nothing be lost.
—Alfred North Whitehead

Almost 2,000 years ago, on the north central coast of Ecuador a small, dark Jama-Coaque Indian took a handful of clay, formed it into a crude human figure, and fired it in his kiln. Perhaps it was a doll for his child, a simple toy, for it wasn't grand or ceremonial, not like the refined figurines of the great artisans of the day. This Indian would die, and the child, too, and the little doll—nothing worth keeping, really—would be lost to the world. Long after the Jama-Coaque tribe ceased to exist, the little doll lay forgotten deep under mud and muck and great heaps of black ash from the great volcanoes in the east.

Then one day, a thousand years ago, an earthquake rattled the entire coast and the monkeys screamed and the jaguars darted off in all directions. The doll found herself unearthed and swimming down the cool rushing river, the winding Rio Jama that empties into the sea. There, in the great, undulating Pacific, she braced herself for the brutal poundings against rock and timber. But she survived, buried in the silky volcanic sand at the bottom of the sea alongside thousands of other Indian clay creations—broken jugs and shattered ceremonial bowls.

But one morning, in the year 1612, she was awakened from her sandy slumber by the cataclysmic sinking of a Spanish Galleon near the mouth of Jama River. It was there that she lost a leg, caught in the groaning movements of that great hulk settling into the watery darkness.

Then, about 400 years later, exhausted by two millennia of being battered and buried and lost to all human contact—for which she was made—she washed up on shore and rested her head against a stone. Sunning herself in the quiet peace of stillness, she was soon noticed by woman taking a walk. She was picked up and much was made of her. She had returned; she was home.

The Past Is with Us

I am that woman-taking-a-walk. I live on the Ecuadorian coast near the Jama River, where shards of pre-Columbian pottery wash ashore with every tide, soon to be reclaimed by the next high tide, that is, if not collected by beachcombers. These pieces of the past continue their endless refrain of coming in and going out—and swirling around that mysterious sandy mound near the mouth of the river, which marks the (yet-to-be excavated) sunken Spanish Galleon. I collect this pottery on daily walks and study the geometric designs characteristic of the Jama-Coaque Indians, a culture which thrived on the banks of the Jama River between 300 B.C.E. to 300 C.E. I love to imagine the people who made the pottery—their lives, their dreams. But when I found the doll, a crudely made human figure, something that might have belonged to a child, I felt something beyond interest; I experienced a profound sense of awe mixed with tenderness.

When I picked up the doll from its resting place against the stone, my immediate thought was this: *Could its creator imagine that 2,000 years later, this very doll—this insignificant creation in the scheme of things—*

would be found and cherished? That made me think about how, in our relational world, the past is always with us; it endures, it persists, it makes the rounds. But it is always there.

Nothing Is Lost

In the process world, every unfolding moment in time is immortal. That means that our tiniest acts, our humblest creations influence the world—not just now, but forever. But how is such immortality possible? To explain, let's assume that the story of the doll's provenance is just as I imagined it.

First, every act finds immortality as it journeys through time. The Indian made a doll for his child, an act of kindness which brings joy to his little girl. This simple act of kindness stimulates the child to act more kindly. One act of kindness stimulates another in numerous expressions and permutations through the child's family, the community, her children's lives, and so on. The act of creating the doll enters the past in what Whitehead calls "objective immortality," continuing its journey of influence, even as it naturally weakens with time. But the influence, even faint, is always there. Even today, the influence of this single creation is part of the enumerable acts of kindness which, like grains of sand that become a beach, build up to define a community, a country, a way of life. That affects me, too, in a very distant way. We know that, in a relational world, even the humblest act of kindness "lives on" and changes the whole configuration of things.

A second way every act finds immortality is within God. In God, the creation of the Jama-Coaque doll is felt fully in its subjective experience: God feels the joy of the child who watches the doll come out of the kiln, the father's pleasure, too. In God, nothing is partial, nothing is past, nothing is lost. Every act is experienced and felt and integrated into God's own "concrescence" or self-creation. In this way we touch God with our kindness, enlivening the divine life with joy. Given God's intimate participation in the creation of the doll, God is then able to offer a novel possibility (the "initial aim") for the next unfolding experience within the natural limitations of the world. In other words, every act of kindness opens up fresh possibilities for the future that may not have been there before.

A Direct Encounter

Immortality can touch us in dramatic ways. There are those special times when the distant past affects us not only through a mediated kind of influence, which weakens with time, but directly. Whitehead believed that it is possible to feel or "prehend" something in the distant past without the usual contiguous, linear mediation described above. After all, the distant past is still here. Sometimes we feel (or "prehend") the distant past with startling clarity. Mystics can attest to this. Psychologists, too. A memory uncovered after years of forgetting may be suddenly unearthed with profound consequences. This may explain, too, instances of "past life" memory. There are those especially sensitive people who may be able to prehend parts of someone else's distant past—a past which still exists—experiencing it as if it were their own.

A direct encounter with the distant past, like finding the ancient doll, gives one a profound sense of connection. We are not God, so we feel the encounter only objectively and partially, not exactly as it happened. Nevertheless, the encounter provokes a sense of awe and wonder and storytelling and imagination; it is an intensely spiritual experience, a numinous moment. This is what happens when we participate in religious ritual. We experience through ritual a more direct connection to the distant past than we do in everyday life. We can feel the past with fresh intensity when listening to a reading from the Torah or partaking of the Eucharist or sitting for meditation. Through myth and symbol and ritual we connect more directly and deeply to the past and to each other—and this, in turn, can bring us closer to the Soul of the Universe, who holds and cherishes and transforms all things with divine loving care.

Everything Matters

In my dumb luck of stumbling upon the pre-Columbian clay figure, I have directly encountered the distant past—at least a piece of it. And that encounter is laced with awe, and even an inkling of the tender feeling that lay behind its creation. I have held the past in my hands. I have taken it home and am changed by the encounter. It has provoked the imaginary story of what might have happened; it has provoked this essay.

The past is still with us, and it possesses power. Everything is past, really, except for the becoming moment. But the distant past can be especially provocative, for it reminds us of our immortality in the world, and of the importance of every action. What we do in the world matters—it matters through the whole trajectory of history; it matters to God, and through God back to the world. And who knows? What we do—the humblest creation, the simplest act of kindness—might just wash up on the shore of some distant generation of awe-struck wanderers.

S-I-Z-I-N-G Up

In a Fat Soul kind of world, small is big. Like the "butterfly effect," small choices, tiny creatures, miniscule gestures of love make a *huge* impact in our interconnected world. And when we are gone, we leave behind a legacy of words, thoughts, and actions that affect the whole, wide universe. We need to leave behind the false notion that we have to do something big and splashy and admired-by-all in order to make a lasting difference. Sometimes those ego-centered goals only lead to disaster. Rather, if we simply make it our goal to increase the size of our souls for the sake of beauty, we will leave behind a lovely, indelible, and unique stamp on the world—a collection of tiny imprints that add hugely to the enjoyment of God.

Heaven, Yes, Heaven

God is the great companion—the fellow-sufferer, who understands.

—Alfred North Whitehead

Market day is a special day on the rural coast of Ecuador. In the nearby town of Jama, just up the hill, our Ecuadorian friend and helper, Primo, starts up the engine on his "mototaxi"—a motorcycle with a bright red open cab attached—to begin his work of transporting people and groceries as very few have cars. Including me. I am his first customer of the day. Primo is short and stocky and strong; he has impeccable manners and a smile that proudly displays a number of silver teeth. Primo's lanky twelve-year-old nephew, Jose, rides along in the cab. This is good. Primo lost his own little boy to an illness a year ago, so the nephew's presence during the school-free months no doubt helps with his grief. Every Tuesday morning, uncle and nephew motor down the winding hill to the tiny fishing village of El Matal. This is where I live.

They collect me at the door of my *casa* with my empty shopping bags, and off we go, the red mototaxi climbing happily back up the hill to the brightly colored fruits and vegetables that await me in Jama. It is a four-mile journey of bliss. The air is sweet and warm—the breeze exquisite. We wind through lush tropical farmland where whole families of lazy cows wander at will; we pass shrimp ponds dotted with snowy egrets—their languorous angelic wings flapping as if in slow motion against misty blue mountains in the distance. It is enough to make the heart full.

Jose, my young riding companion, has warm brown skin, delicate features, and thick, longish hair. He sits in the front seat of his uncle's cab while I sit behind, where there is more leg room. For the fifteen-minute journey to Jama, Jose and I casually teach each other words from our own languages, but Jose does most of the teaching. He points to the snowy egrets and says *ave blanca* (white bird) and I repeat it back. Then we pass grazing cows on the hillside and I learn *vacas* (cows). Jose laughs at my accent—we both do, as I am new at this language game.

When we arrive in Jama, Jose and I climb down from the mototaxi near the fresh vegetable stand on the street. Jose points out vegetables and fruits, naming them in Spanish, and making sure the vendor does her job efficiently—and more importantly, that I am not overcharged. He carries the overflowing produce bag back to the mototaxi, and off we go to the mom and pop store for staples. Despite his skinny frame, Jose carries everything himself, no matter how heavy; he insists. We cross the street. Other mototaxis whizz by, and Jose puts out an arm to stop me from stepping out in front of them. I buy Jose a Coca-Cola, and he accepts it with a smile and a shy *gracias*.

We have a system—Jose and I—a relationship, a way of doing things, and it feels good. I look forward to seeing Jose's smile on market days and wonder what new words we will learn together.

One day, the mototaxi pulls up to my home, but Jose is missing. Primo has brought his wife, Marguerite, instead, and they both look uncharacteristically distressed, as if something is wrong. I naturally ask about Jose, and they take turns, speaking fast and furiously with dramatic gesturing, as Latins are prone to do. The only word I actually understand is "Jose." Something about Jose. Something is *wrong* with Jose. But nothing could possibly be wrong with Jose, I tell myself, or at least nothing serious. He is a healthy twelve-year-old, full of life and energy and curiosity. So I interpret their incomprehensible Spanish and wild gesturing in my own preferred way: Jose has had some kind of accident and has broken something, possibly an arm, from what I could make out. It saddens me to think of it, but boys do that—they break bones; it happens. I offer a heartfelt "*Lo siento*" (I'm sorry) as I climb aboard the mototaxi, and vow inwardly to spend more time on my Spanish.

When we arrive in Jama, I ask Primo to stop at a special little shop (*tienda*) that carries games and gifts for children. I purchase a Bingo game, very nice, but a little expensive. When I take the game back to the mototaxi and hand it to Primo with the words *para Jose* (for Jose), Primo's expressive face suddenly freezes, the Bingo game stranded awkwardly between us. He glances at his wife, as if for help. Marguerite gently takes the game and tucks it under the seat of the mototaxi, out of sight. We move on.

A stab of fear shoots through me—could Jose be that bad off? I brush the thought away, thinking that I must have made a cultural *faux pas*. Yes, that's it. Perhaps you can't give presents like this. And surely, I reasoned, Primo and his wife would not be helping me today if something terrible had happened.

One week later, the red mototaxi appears at my door as usual, this time with a grown man as passenger, sitting exactly where Jose usually sits. He is a handsome man, dark and quiet. His hair is cut short and neat. Primo introduces him as Jose's papa. I ask after Jose— "*¿Como está Jose?*" (How is Jose?)—at least I know how to do this. Again, I get a puzzled, frozen look from Primo, and now the same look from the father.

This is too much. I throw my arms out in a pleading gesture and cry, "*No entiendo!*" (I don't understand!) My rigid denial—hiding behind a huge language barrier—begins to wobble. I am listening now, really listening. Primo keeps talking, this time more slowly. He is kind; he wants me to understand. I catch a word—finally, a word I understand—but oh, how I wish I did not understand! The word is *muerto*. Dead. I repeat it back in disbelief, and Primo slowly nods. My hand flies to my heart as I take a step back. "No," I say. "No!"

I pull out my cell phone and call a translator that I use only for emergencies. After the translator talks to Primo, I take the phone, my hand shaking. The sober voice of the translator confirms that the boy was killed over a week ago in a tragic accident. Jose is dead. He has been dead all this time.

Primo and Jose's papa try to comfort *me*, this overwrought *gringa*, slow on the uptake, while they are suffering grief beyond my imagination.

In robotic fashion, I climb aboard. They came all the way from Jama; I cannot disappoint. We trundle up the hill in the red mototaxi, now a sorrowful mototaxi: a ponderous conveyance bearing the heavy weight of our grief—the three of us, silently united by this terrible knowledge.

When we reach the *tienda* where I buy my eggs and staples, I feel disoriented and dizzy by the crowd—so many customers and too many voices, loud and cheerful. I squat down to the low shelf where the brown eggs are lined up in neat rows. I place each egg carefully into my own cardboard carton, one by one, until I have a full dozen. I rise and turn, trembling with thoughts of a little boy who loved snowy egrets and cows and school-free days, and who laughed at my funny accent. Suddenly, I realize that the carton of eggs is no longer in my hands but on the floor, the entire dozen broken and yellow and running into the dusty grout like rivers of sorrow. Customers halt and stare. I stand immobile, transfixed, watching the spread of waste, noting the odd contours of brokenness through irrepressible tears. The store owner appears with a broom and a smile of reassurance. She cannot understand my weeping over broken eggs, and I cannot explain it.

On the way home, I gather myself, remembering my companions who sit stoically in front of me. Here is Primo, who has lost not only his son one year ago, but now his nephew. I think of Jose's papa, who rides along with his brother-in-law, not saying much, just rides along—maybe, I think, because the driver knows his pain from the inside; he is in the presence of a fellow-sufferer, who understands.

In the silence, it dawns on me that I might at least say something of comfort to the father, using what little Spanish I can muster. My mind flounders for a word, anything, however inadequate. Then I remember a vocabulary word I recently learned: *cielo* (heaven). Supposing my companions are Catholic, I risk it: *"Jose está en cielo."* (Jose is in heaven.) Jose's papa offers a single nod, his stoic face softens; a flash of something appears in the dark wells of his eyes. *"Cielo,"* he echoes, his tone reverential. Primo, listening from the driver's seat, turns back and says, as if it were a benediction, *"Cielo. Si, cielo."* (Heaven. Yes, heaven.)

The musical sound of the word *cielo*, spoken aloud by each of us, adds a tender element to the air, to the scenery, to the ache itself.

As silence descends again, a profound respect for my traveling companions wells up inside me. I observe Primo as he drives with his usual care—quiet, composed, focused on his task. Jose's papa gazes thoughtfully out at the hills, the banana plants, and the young papaya trees. I think to myself: Heaven holds them together; heaven makes daily work possible; heaven keeps the molecules of their bodies from flying apart.

As the mototaxi winds back down the hill through the verdant landscape, alive with the same beauty that welcomed us when Jose was alive, we pass the snow-white egrets with their enormous, graceful wings; we pass the quiet shrimp ponds that mirror softly shaped hills; we pass the lumbering cows—a baby calf nursing—and I feel the Heart of the whole world, breaking: It breaks over the beauty, it breaks under the sky, it breaks into rivers of sorrow and hope. It breaks clear through the paper wall that separates heaven and earth.

S-I-Z-I-N-G Up

The Celtic tradition tells us that Heaven and Earth are only three feet apart, and that in special places, called "thin places," heaven and earth seem to nearly collapse into each other. When this happens, we can see through the thin veil into the largeness and holiness of the cosmos. Theologian Bruce Epperly says that "a thin place joins heaven and earth, time and eternity, body and spirit, and God and the world."[65] In my own experience, "thin places" are inhabited by snowy egrets and memories of little boys who loved them. Could it be that beauty is the very door to heaven? Whatever our various views of the afterlife, perhaps the beauty of this world can nourish an Earth filled with Heaven.

On the Road Again

The only people for me are the mad ones, the ones who are mad to live, mad to talk, mad to be saved, desirous of everything at the same time, the ones who never yawn or say a commonplace thing, but burn, burn, burn like fabulous yellow roman candles exploding like spiders across the stars.

—Jack Kerouac

On the road again—
just can't wait to get on the road again,
The life I love is making music with my friends . . .
—Willie Nelson, "On the Road Again"

These days, my head is filled with the gravelly voice of Willie Nelson singing "On the Road Again." We are alike, Willie and I, and not just because of our long hair; like Willie, I am constantly on the road. While I fantasize about living in some ancestral home, sipping tea next to a wall of old books and only going places in my head, life hasn't exactly worked out that way. There's the Willie-in-me to contend with: edgy, discontent, succumbing to novelty and Blue Skies.

But then, bohemianism runs through my veins. My great-grandmother Schwartz was literally from Bohemia (today, the Czech Republic). She immigrated to America, married outside her faith to a Jewish immigrant, staked out land in her covered wagon during the Oklahoma Land Run, built a hotel beside freshly laid train tracks, and sold diamonds to weary—not to mention, wary—travelers.   Jack Kerouac would have loved her.   Lizzie Schwartz was a renegade, one of the "mad ones," and definitely a hippie before her time. But not out of preference. Her husband died early on, leaving her with twin boys and not much else, so everything she did, she did for survival.   The stories about Lizzie Schwartz—this counter-cultural, formidable, brilliantly resourceful woman—must have seeped into my soul when I wasn't looking.

In the spirit of my Bohemian great-grandmother, along with Willie Nelson, Jack Kerouac, and a long list of other bohemian-types, I'm about ready to hit the road again. Having sojourned in Ecuador for five unsettling, gorgeous, and sometimes terrifying years, we (my bohemian husband, my bohemian cat, and I) are going back to "the old country" (USA) to begin yet another adventure. It feels a bit mad.

Lest you think Willie and I have even more in common, I can't say that I smoke weed, but I do inhale ideas and beauty and rich experiences with a gusto that approaches a "high."   Such is the life of a Fat Soul philosopher. Despite the difficulties of a pioneer life in a strange land, I must admit that my time in Ecuador has nevertheless been a fertile moment for my work—a sort of lifeline, to be honest. Perhaps that's because as Madeline L'Engle said, "**Our truest response to the irrationality of the world is to paint or sing or write, for only in such responses do we find truth.**"

During times of intense stress—like when we were mugged on the street or when we lost electricity for days or when our home was about to be washed away in the monster tides—the one thing that kept me from flying off the earth in all directions was my spiritual foundation that seemed to be more solid than real life. That is, I developed over the course of my time in Ecuador an undaunted belief in going wide, going deep, going incessantly and lovingly toward beauty. Every moment is new. Every suffering can be transformed. It is a kind of interior traveling that keeps moving forward, come what may. I have found that having a philosophy of life that works when the chips are down makes the difference between sheer waste and tragic beauty, between going small and going wide, between wilting in despair and creating out of chaos.

As I write this, days before our homeward journey begins, I think about the people in California and Washington who have lost their homes in raging wildfires. I worry about the Syrian refugees who are running for their lives. I remember all the immigrants who find refuge in my country—and of my own immigrant ancestors who longed to feel welcomed in an unwelcoming world. The urge for home, for stability, for a sense of belonging haunts all of us who are constantly on the road, but especially those whose journey is a life-or-death ordeal. In an age of climate change, there will be no end to refugees "on the road" for sheer survival.

But my philosophy tells me that, in a sense, we are all on the road, for we are all changing or in the midst of change, and that's okay. We just have to do our best and take care of one another and find comfort in beauty. I remember my great-grandmother's diamonds, the ones she offered to train-travelers. It reminds me that each of us is a tiny, brilliant diamond in Indra's Net of Jewels: an enormous, intricately woven, web-like cosmos in which each eye of the net hosts a beautiful jewel reflecting the whole. This is our universe. We're all in this together. And when we understand that, we can be "at home" wherever we happen to be.

Fat Soul philosophy makes room for faith, too— not faith in a small, mean, all-controlling, black-and-white, Us-vs.-Them sort of deity (so popular these days!), but rather in the less fashionable Fat-Soul-kind-of-God: the God of enormous Soul, the God of love—a divinity intertwined with the world and its sufferings—a God who, at least from my own tradition, looks a lot like Jesus. And that is how my husband and I have survived our own losses, fears, and misadventures in a foreign country. We are empowered by a sense that at the bottom of all the chaos, there lies an unswerving Tenderness: the very

Soul of the world, who inhabits our suffering, who creates out of chaos, and who cannot get along very well without us. Because that is the nature of love.

So I grab my hat and hit the road again in search of a new home. But I leave Ecuador with only a small sense of loss and a huge sense of gain—for I have gained girth in my soul. At least for now. Tomorrow I could be a cringing mess. It's a process. The soul-expanding journey unfolds like jazz, like improvisation, like music-on-the-road. Every moment is a new becoming. As the philosopher Bob Mesle says, "the future does not exist," and thank God for that, for a future-not-yet-written is a future filled with hope.

And wherever I end up, I know I will still be "on the road" metaphorically speaking: becoming new each moment, making the music of Fat Soul, fleshing out new thoughts, meeting new Fat Souls from around the world, sharing ideas, and working together toward a more broad-minded, large-souled world—"our common home," as Pope Francis reminds us. It's like a high, like music, like a band of Fat Souls of every religion and tradition and culture all improvising together in beautifully imperfect harmony. And what could be better than making music with our friends?

S-I-Z-I-N-G Up

We inhabit a world of becomings, whether or not we see ourselves in motion or at rest, in transition or in peaceful quietude. It's all journey, it's all in process. And that means there is always freshness afoot in the world. In our fears about the future—terrorism, global warming, war and famine—we can live in hope. Not pretend hope or naïve hope or false hope, but actual, authentic hope. Each moment is ripe with fresh possibility. Whitehead describes Peace as "trust in the efficacy of Beauty." In these challenging times when the whole world seems to be in a cataclysmic transition, may our souls fling wide toward trust, toward beauty, toward each other, toward hope. We are not alone.

Epilogue

Fat Soul in Process

Philosophy is born of wonder; it is the art of wondering in a disciplined, thoughtful way.
—C. Robert Mesle

From wonder into wonder, existence opens.
—Lao Tzu

Everyone is a philosopher of sorts. You, me, the guy next door. Everyone. We might not crack open thick books by Kant and Hegel and Marx and write papers about ontology and epistemology, but still, we wonder. We wonder about the world, and we make assumptions. We listen to our favorite band and mull over the lyrics. We might even pretend to be the lead singer—and wonder what it would be like to sing out our thoughts and be adored by the masses. And that makes us wonder about the meaning of it all. All this. What's the purpose? Love? Sex? Money? Beauty?

Yes, we are natural wonderers, picking up ideas from everywhere and filing them away, however haphazardly. We all have a philosophy-of-sorts going on in our heads, whether we are conscious of it or not. The actual study of philosophy helps us do our wondering "in a disciplined, thoughtful way." There's something to be said for that. Not everybody is into that sort of thing, of course, but some of us nerd-types can actually enjoy the discipline of philosophy and discover that it might—dare I say it?—even be *useful* in the real world.

But what if I'm religious? Doesn't philosophy destroy religious belief? It can. But philosophy can also be a good friend to faith if we dare to allow ourselves a little space in our souls for wonder. For example, each of us comes to a religious text or tradition wearing philosophical glasses: assumptions we hold about the world and about the people and animals that make it up. That's why people who read the same sacred text can end up a Pat Robertson or a Mother Theresa, a Hitler or a Martin Luther King, Jr. It's all about what you bring to your religion, that is, those hidden assumptions created by your cultural and psychological influences, your prejudices and traumas, your understanding of power and relationships and meaning.

So, becoming aware of the assumptions that color our religion and the way we treat others and our planet is a good thing. That's where philosophy comes in: it helps clarify and integrate our knowledge, experience, and religiosity. Philosophy can shine a light on our theology—that is, our ideas about God and the world. After all, many of our theological assumptions come to us via the great philosophers of the past. Many of their ideas were good ones; others, not so much—or at least, severely outdated.

For some people, philosophy can even bring about belief. Take me, for instance. I'm probably one of the few people in the history of higher education who lost my faith as a result of studying theology at a seminary and gained my faith as result of studying philosophy at a secular university.

My Journey

During my seminary studies at a large (but slim-thinking) seminary, I could never get past "the problem of evil and suffering," so after graduation my traditional Christian faith took a reluctant nosedive into agnosticism. I could not, in good conscience, believe in God in the face of horrible realities like the Holocaust and Vietnam. After poring over all the traditional "theodicies" that try to justify belief in a traditional God—i.e., an all-powerful, all-good God—my search finally came to a dead end. My spiritual life became one huge sigh of regret. Why did I have to think so much? What was wrong with me?

Since I was already an agnostic, I figured I might as well go all the way and join other skeptics and seekers. That's when I took up the study of philosophy in the graduate program at the University of Missouri and became a teaching assistant. One day, as I was preparing to teach a philosophy class, one of my professors handed me a copy of a journal article by Charles Hartshorne about the British philosopher Alfred North Whitehead's view of God and the world. I devoured the article and signed up for a seminar on Whitehead. It was the beginning of my life-long love affair with process thought.

As a spiritual person by nature, I was especially intrigued by Whitehead's "poet of the world" concept of God, a relational God, a God defined by love rather than power, a concept of God which cut against the grain of the traditional view of God defined by Western philosophy (and duly adopted by Western theologians). In the traditional Greek-inspired view, God holds all power in the universe (omnipotence), while love is only an attribute. But Whitehead turns the whole unseemly idea of omnipotence—that tragic flaw of Western thought—on its head, and comes across more like the New Testament writer of 1 John who stated flatly, "God is love." Omnipotence was demolished—as dead and gone as Hitler and Mussolini—in this radically organic philosophy of shared power or what philosopher Bernard Loomer called "relational power" as opposed to "unilateral power." And out of the ashes of omnipotence emerged the power of love and beauty and the possibilities for freshness and hope in each unfolding new moment. This rocked my world.

The Power of Love

In Whitehead's thought (and quantum physics) everything is connected—everything—and for Whitehead, that includes God. God is not up in the sky running things like a dispassionate CEO (with highly questionable morals). Instead, God "dwells in the tender elements in the world, which slowly and in quietness operate by love."[66]

This is not pantheism, which would say God and the world are the same thing, but rather, pan*en*theism: God inhabits every nook and cranny of the world and yet is more than the world. So our values, which are rooted in our view of God, begin to switch from the love of power to the power of love. Theologian David Polk describes this view of God quite elegantly as "the God of empowering love."[67]

The power of love and the teleology of beauty take center stage in Whitehead's process philosophy. Every moment is new, and every response is free—free to either diminish ourselves or enlarge ourselves. It is truly a F.A.T. Soul philosophy built on ideas of Flexibility, Aesthetics, and Tenderness. Process philosophy tells us that we are all in this together—you, me, the ceibo tree, God—all of us. And that is good news! Process theologian Bruce Epperly calls this interdependent state of affairs "a holy adventure."[68] Adventure indeed—right down to the quotidian. For we are co-creators, where every choice we make, every smile or angry outburst or act of kindness or ill-conceived action makes an impact on the world and on God. The implications of this "shared power" kind of universe for spirituality, community, relationships, global warming, and personal responsibility are staggering.

As for my own journey, a Whiteheadian view of God was only part of my personal "Copernican Revolution." Whitehead's radically open and interconnected view of the universe—a monumental break with Cartesian dualism—also made sense to me in light of quantum science. Everything made sense on a profound level, not just my relationship with God, but my relationship with snowy egrets and tree frogs and bees. I no longer had to choose between science and religion— what a relief!

Finally, after indulging in books by process theologians in my own tradition, I was able to return to the idea of religion—albeit with a radically new understanding of God and the world. I eventually became a minister in a progressive Christian denomination and introduced my husband, a professor of religious studies, to Whitehead's thought. He ended up writing a seminal work on process hermeneutics.[69]

The Big Tent Philosophy

But Whitehead's philosophy, or process philosophy, is not just for Christians-in-crisis—not by a long shot. Some of the finest process theologians today are Jewish (e.g., Rabbi Bradley Shavit Artson). Many traditions East and West are currently in dialogue with Whitehead—Buddhism for example, which, like process thought, has always been a relational, interconnected way of seeing the world. Buddhism makes sense in light of process thought—a great deal of sense. In China today, with its event-oriented language and rich philosophical history, Whitehead's thought is blossoming. Process thought is a big-tent philosophy for anyone of any faith—and for naturalists, environmentalists, and those who have an understanding of spirituality that stands outside of any particular religious tradition.

Process philosophy—the inspiration for Fat Soul—allows me to embrace my own tradition even while I deepen my appreciation for other spiritual paths. Diversity enriches, making our own spiritual path more beautiful. Once we see that we are all shimmering facets in a bejeweled net-like universe, we begin to reach out to people of other worldviews and religions and seek to understand and be enriched. In a nutshell, process thought engenders empathy. So beware of becoming a process thinker! You will be infused with—and challenged by—*empathy,* and that changes everything.

For process philosophy is all about expanding our souls to embrace contrasts and differences in a richly interwoven world that is always in the process of becoming. It's about seeking beauty in our relationships, not only with people who are different from us, but with animals and the planet and the very air we breathe. And in this world of religious conflict and environmental disaster, such a philosophy as Whitehead's—one which promotes beauty and justice and relational harmony among all living beings—well, it couldn't hurt, could it?

Fat Soul: Taking It to the Streets

The metaphor of Fat Soul reminds us, too, that in a process world with no more metaphysical dualisms to contend with, spirituality is free to get fat: to widen out beyond the psyche to embrace the body, the soil, the land, and the whole wide, gorgeous planet. This means that philosophy should never remain a cerebral exercise. It is by nature, ecological.

The Whiteheadian tradition is an ever-expanding, open-ended tradition, full of great thinkers and scholars who are doing marvelous things in the world. One of these process philosophers, the late Bernard Loomer, believed that when it comes to the soul, S-I-Z-E matters. This more soulful aspect is not just tangential, but challenges philosophy, a discipline which tends to remain contentedly seated somewhere in the mind, to transcend itself, to get up and move out in all directions. Here is where Fat Soul can help. Fat Soul philosophy reaches up to the grand ideas floating about in the rarified air of academia and brings them down into the realm of poetry and poverty, beauty and heartbreak, music and storytelling—a full-bodied embrace of our gorgeous and terrifying world.

My collaborator in the development of Fat Soul, Professor Jay McDaniel of Hendrix College, is taking process philosophy out for a walk in the real world, working to apply the many dimensions of Fat Soul thinking to both the classroom and the community. As a musician, he has created the Fat Soul Band and a Fat Soul network of musicians in Central Arkansas. With the support of the Reverend Teri Daily and the St. Peter's

Episcopal Church in Conway, Arkansas, he has created Fat Soul Festivals celebrating ecology and multicultural dialogue. Dr. McDaniel also works each year with China's Center for Constructive Postmodernism, using ideas from process/Fat Soul philosophy to help promote sustainable communities and multi-cultural dialogue in that country. Dr. McDaniel says that process philosophy needs to move beyond mere worldview, and asserts that the "age of disembodied ideas" is over.

> Yes, process philosophy is indeed influenced by the cosmology of Whitehead with its emphasis on interconnectedness and the intrinsic value of all living beings. In this sense it is a metaphysics. But its aim is not to enframe the world and denude it of its mystery and beauty; and process philosophy makes no claim to finality of statement. Its aim instead is to guide us into a kinder and more creative way of living in the world with help from many other sources: religious, scientific, artistic, and ethical. Process philosophy is now a lifestyle and an attitude toward life, not just a worldview. It is a lifestyle and attitude the world sorely needs if our souls are to widen and our hearts are to open, for the sake of the well-being of people, animals, and the earth.[70]

With this in mind, Fat Soul philosophy can be viewed as process philosophy intentionally embodied—and even transcended for the sake of the world. This means that while process philosophy gave birth to Fat Soul philosophy, not all in the Fat Soul community are process thinkers in any formal sense. Many in the Fat Soul community (which we now call Fat Soul International) are poets and artists and musicians and librarians and engineers and activists and college students who are working out their own philosophy of life with the help of Fat Soul ideas and attitudes as portrayed in our "manifesto" below.

We hope that whatever tradition you come from, you will join our Fat Soul community as we expand outward in all directions with our stubborn, undaunted hope of creating a more joyful world that values beauty and kindness, a world that is sustainable and just—or least a world that is moving, in fits and starts, in that general direction.

For Further Expansion

Fat Soul International: A Manifesto

By Patricia Adams Farmer and Jay McDaniel

In a world filled with rigidity in the forms of religious fundamentalism, racism, injustice, planetary destruction, xenophobia, and panphobia—yes, the Fear of Everything—there is an alternative: the way of FAT SOUL.

We believe that instead of shrinking back in despair or approaching the world with raised hackles, we need to widen out in love, compassion, inclusivity, and full-bodied joy. This unseemly business of widening out when everyone else is shrinking back may seem wildly counter-cultural, but it just might relieve some of the angst of these troubled times.

And it could even—yes, if we get fat enough—change the world.

What is a Fat Soul? Just what it sounds like. Fat Souls are wide souls, expansive souls—souls too big to fit into the slim-cut "Us" and "Them" categories. Fat Soul is a philosophy of life, a kind of wide-angle lens through which to see life, community, and the Big Wide World.

Our goal is to draw the circle of compassion wider.

We are philosophers, teachers, theologians, guitarists, singers, dancers, poets, gardeners, accountants, artists, and spiritually interested people from around the world who believe, that when it comes to the soul, size matters.

We are Fat Soul International.

Fat Soul International does not belong to one faith or spiritual path. You can be a Fat Soul Christian or a Fat Soul Jew or a Fat Soul Muslim or a Fat Soul Buddhist or a Fat Soul Hindu or a Fat Soul Naturalist or a Spiritual-But-Not-Religious Fat Soul. We believe that no matter who you are, if you're expanding in compassion rather than shrinking back in fear, you're going in the right direction.

Fat Souls do not seek after neat-and-tidy sameness or shallow harmony, but enjoy the messy complexity which makes life vivid and true and beautiful.

We who seek to become Fat Souls love beauty; we love the earth. We love sustainable communities. We love metaphor, too. We see ourselves as diverse facets of a bejeweled universe, reflecting one another with humility, respect, and hospitality. We see ourselves as part of the earth, part of each other, part of the stars.

Here are some things we believe and that are important to us:

We believe in the power of kindness.

We believe that small is big: small choices, tiny creatures, and miniscule gestures of love make a huge impact in our interconnected world.

We know that to become Fat Souls, we need to say no to things that impoverish not only our own souls, but the souls of others on this planet. Protest can be good.

We believe in robust individuality, but not selfish individualism. We are all connected.

We see the value of not only moving out in expansion, but of contracting from time to time for self-reflection. A soulful life is a balanced life.

We see full well the absurdities and evils of our time. Yet, we are not cynics. We believe in hope. We believe in deep listening. We believe that mirth makes girth; laughter makes us larger.

We refuse to be abstemious in our thinking or rigid in our rules or stingy with our compassion.

We value the widening wisdom of age and experience.

We value mindfulness. We reserve our fear for saber-tooth tigers.

We work for social and economic justice. We stand with the poor, and expand our imaginations toward their well-being.

We stand with our fellow creatures who inhabit our planet, and that includes farm animals.

We stand with the earth itself and consider it part of our own soul; we vow to protect it as we do the people we love.

We believe in the power of music and art and creative work of all kinds.

We do not have all the answers and are, without apology, open-ended in our thinking.

Yes, we are people of all religions and cultures and colors and sizes and body-types and ages and sexual orientation; we are extroverts and introverts; we are artists and engineers; we are those who sing the blues and those who sing arias; we are those who love chocolate and those (unfortunates) who do not.

So, you see, we're talking largesse here, huge and spacious souls who cover a vast terrain, transcending all national borders and political ideologies, all growing larger and more intensely harmonious by our very diversity. Together we stretch our imaginations and talents toward increasing the amount of kindness in the world. We embrace the full catastrophe of life and know that it can be transformed.

In a nutshell, we are a network of networks of networks of people around the world who seek to live with compassion and creativity, open-heartedness and open-mindedness. We are Fat Soul International.

Will you join us? Here's how to do it.

Begin by blooming where you're planted. In your own local community, create Fat Soul Festivals and Fat Soul Farmer's Markets and Fat Soul Book Discussions and Fat Soul Bands. Do it as a community effort and know that you are linked with people in other parts of the world who are doing these things, too.

Also you can be part of our Fat Soul International community by doing quiet things like writing Fat Soul poems, or taking Fat Soul naps, or meditating, or caring for homeless animals, or worshipping with your faith community, or talking one-on-one about Fat Soul ideas over cups of tea. All of this matters hugely in our interconnected world.

* * *

Whatever your Fat Soul style, if you resonate with this manifesto, we invite you to visit our ever-expanding Fat Soul resources (including a Chinese translation of the Manifesto) at:

- *Fat Soul International* website
  (www.fatsoul.org)
- Patricia Adams Farmer's website
  (www.patriciaadamsfarmer.com)
- *Jesus, Jazz, and Buddhism: Process Thinking for a More Hospitable World*
  (www.jesusjazzbuddhism.org)

If you're on Facebook, be sure to join our *Fat Soul Café* group where we offer a varied menu of soul-nourishing ideas, share Fat Soul community happenings, and make Fat Soul Friends from around the world.

About the Author

Patricia Adams Farmer is a featured writer for *Jesus, Jazz, and Buddhism: Process Thinking for a More Hospitable World.* She is the author of *Embracing a Beautiful God* (now in a tenth anniversary edition), editor of *Replanting Ourselves in Beauty: Toward an Ecological Civilization* (with Jay McDaniel), and author of two novels, *The Metaphor Maker* and *Fat Soul Fridays.* With an undergraduate degree in music and graduate degrees in philosophy, theology, and education, she was ordained into the Christian Church (Disciples of Christ) and served as pastor for churches in Ohio and California. Later, she taught Independent Studies for at-risk high school students in Tustin, California. After a five-year adventure in Ecuador, she and her husband Ron Farmer now reside in Albuquerque, New Mexico. Visit her website at www.patriciaadamsfarmer.com.

Endnotes

1 Elizabeth Gilbert, *Big Magic: Creative Living Beyond Fear (Riverhead Books),* Kindle Electronic Edition, Location 2439.

2 Jay McDaniel and Patricia Adams Farmer, editors, *Replanting Ourselves in Beauty: Toward an Ecological Civilization* (Process Century Press, 2015).

3 Bernard Loomer, "S-I-Z-E Is the Measure," in Harry James Cargas and Bernard Lee, eds., *Religious Experience and Process Theology* (Paulist Press, 1976). Also see "Two Conceptions of Power," *Process Studies* 6:1 (1976).

4 Jay McDaniel, "Crazier Than Hell: A Whiteheadian Appreciation of Shamanism," *Jesus, Jazz, and Buddhism: Process Thinking for a More Hospitable World*. Web.

5 Bob Mesle, "A Soul Is Not a Thing," *Jesus, Jazz, and Buddhism: Process Thinking for a More Hospitable World*. Web.

6 Patricia Adams Farmer, *Fat Soul Fridays* (Estrella de Mar Publications, 2013), 108.

7 Alfred North Whitehead, *Adventures of Ideas* (New York: The Free Press, 1961), 265.

8 Alfred North Whitehead, *Process and Reality*, corrected ed., eds. David Ray Griffin and Donald W, Sherburne (New York: The Free Press, 1978), 343.

9 Ibid., 351.

10 David P. Polk, *God of Empowering Love: A History and Reconception of the Theodicy Conundrum* (Process Century Press, forthcoming).

11 Alexander McCall Smith, *Comforts of a Muddy Saturday: An Isabel Dalhousie Novel,* Kindle Electronic Edition, Location 2044.

12 Whitehead, *Process and Reality*, 346.

13 Ibid., 351.

14 Bradley Shavit Artson, *God of Becoming and Relationship: The Dynamic Nature of Process Theology* (Jewish Lights, 2013), Kindle Electronic Edition, Location 1375.

15 Richard R. Powell, *Wabi Sabi Simple: Create Beauty. Value Imperfection. Live Deeply.* (Adams Media, 2004).

16 Whitehead, *Process and Reality*, 39.

17 Susan Cain, *Quiet: The Power of Introverts in a World That Can't Stop Talking* (Crown Publishing, 2012), Kindle Electronic Edition.

[18] Ibid, Location 537.

[19] Ibid, Location 1836.

[20] Whitehead, *Process and Reality*, 343.

[21] Whitehead, *Adventures of Ideas*, 296.

[22] Rachel Carson, *The Sense of Wonder* (HarperCollins, 1998).

[23] Jay McDaniel, "Our Delightfully Imperfect Pope," *Jesus, Jazz, and Buddhism: Process Thinking for a More Hospitable World.* Web.

[24] Jay McDaniel, "Twenty Key Ideas in Process Thought," *Jesus, Jazz, and Buddhism: Process Thinking for a More Hospitable World.* Web.

[25] See David Ray Griffin, ed., *The Reenchantment of Science: Postmodern Proposals* (Albany: SUNY Press, 1988) and other volumes in the SUNY series, Constructive Postmodern Thought, edited by Griffin.

[26] Ronald L. Farmer, "Imagination and The Art of Interpretation: Reading Scripture and Tradition for the Sake of the World," *Replanting Ourselves in Beauty: Toward an Ecological Civilization,* eds. Jay McDaniel and Patricia Adams Farmer (Process Century Press, 2015), 128.

[27] Harish, "How Many Animals Does a Vegetarian Save?" *Counting Animals.* Web.

[28] Whitehead, *Process and Reality*, 105.

[29] Whitehead, *Adventures of Ideas*, 285.

[30] Vincent van Gogh, Letter 133, cited in Cliff Edwards, *Van Gogh and God: A Creative Spiritual Quest* (Chicago: Loyola University Press), 54.

[31] Edwards, *Van Gogh and God*, 69.

[32] Vincent van Gogh, Letter 625, cited in Edwards, *Van Gogh and God*, 57.

[33] Vincent van Gogh, Letter, 161, cited in Edwards, *Van Gogh and God*, 51.

[34] Patricia Adams Farmer, "Van Gogh's God," in *Embracing a Beautiful God: Tenth Anniversary Edition* (Estrella de Mar Publications), 122-24.

[35] Whitehead, *Adventures of Ideas*, 266.

[36] Ibid.

[37] Don McLean, "Starry Night," *Vincent* single, 1971.

[38] Whitehead, *Adventures of Ideas*, 296.

[39] Austen Ivereigh, *The Great Reformer: Francis and the Making of a Radical Pope* (Henry Holt), Kindle Electronic Edition, Location 349.

[40] Whitehead, *Process and Reality*, 351.

[41] Robert Schuman, quoted in "Mozart's Last Symphony: The Giant 'Jupiter,'" *All Things Considered*, Elizabeth Blair, NPR, January 27, 2006.

[42] Peter Shaffer, *Amadeus* (1979).

43 Whitehead, *Process and Reality*, 343.

44 Robert Levin, "Mozart's Last Symphony: The Giant 'Jupiter,'" *All Things Considered*, Elizabeth Blair, NPR, January 27, 2006.

45 Woody Allen, "Mozart's Last Symphony: The Giant 'Jupiter,'" *All Things Considered*, Elizabeth Blair, NPR, January 27, 2006.

46 Whitehead, *Adventures of Ideas*, viii.

47 Volume III of *The Library of Living Philosophers*, edited by P. A. Schilpp.

48 Quoted in Richard Lubbock, "Philosophy for the Muddleheaded." *Sympatico*. Web.

49 Ibid.

50 Ibid.

51 Whitehead, *Process and Reality*, 346.

52 Whitehead, *Adventure of Ideas*, 296.

53 Cited by Elizabeth Gilbert, *Big Magic*, Kindle Electronic Edition, Location 73.

54 Malala Yousafzai, interview, *The Andrew Marr Show*, BBC, October 13, 2013.

55 Jay McDaniel, "Sunlight, Moonlight, and the Craziness of God," *Jesus, Jazz, and Buddhism*. Web.

56 Ibid.

57 David A. Graham, "The Excellent Paradox of Dave Brubeck," *The Atlantic*. Web.

58 Josh Rothman, "Profiles, Dave Brubeck," *The New Yorker*. Web.

59 Elaine Woo, "Youngest on Schindler's List," *Los Angeles Times*. Web.

60 Jay McDaniel, *Living from the Center: Spirituality in an Age of Consumerism* (St. Louis: Chalice Press, 2000), 121-22, 25.

61 Jay McDaniel, "Crystal Bridges Museum and the Dazzling Effect," *Jesus, Jazz, and Buddhism*. Web.

62 Marjorie Hewitt Suchocki, *In God's Presence: Theological Reflections on Prayer* (St. Louis: Chalice Press, 1996), 66.

63 Robinson Jeffers, "The Eye," *Selected Poems* (New York: Vintage Books, 1963), 85.

64 Bob Mesle, "The Future Does Not Exist," *Jesus, Jazz, and Buddhism*. Web.

65 Bruce Epperly, Personal Correspondence, Aug. 3, 2015.

66 Whitehead, *Process and Reality*, 343.

67 Polk, *God of Empowering Love*.

68 Bruce Epperly, *Holy Adventure: 41 Days of Audacious Living* (Parson's Porch and Co., 2014).

69 Ronald L. Farmer, *Beyond the Impasse: The Promise of a Process Hermeneutic* (Macon: Mercer University Press, 1997).

70 Jay McDaniel, "Fat Soul Century: All Are Welcome," *Jesus, Jazz, and Buddhism*. Web.

Lightning Source UK Ltd.
Milton Keynes UK
UKHW03f0418120318
319267UK00008B/195/P